SEN
BAZ
URU

S E N
B A Z
U R U

SMALL STEPS TO HOPE,
HEALING AND HAPPINESS

MICHAEL JAMES WONG

Illustrated by Niki Priest

MICHAEL  JOSEPH

Mindfulness is the art of living in the moment, the willingness to slow down and become completely present, on purpose, without judgement, as each moment unfolds.

Folding paper is a beautiful practice of mindfulness, if you allow it to be.

This is the gift of Senbazuru.

In Japan, the paper crane is a symbol of peace, hope and healing. Considered the bird of happiness, this mystical and majestic creature is believed to live for a thousand years and, according to tradition, if a person were to fold one thousand paper cranes in a single year, they would be granted a single wish, one that could bring good fortune, eternal luck, long life and happiness.

The undertaking of folding one thousand cranes is no small task; courage, dedication and purpose is required. Every fold is deliberate and considerate, each crane inspired and resilient. It is a journey of hope, commitment and exploration, forgiveness and, in the end, joy.

Through folding one thousand paper cranes it is believed that we discover our own path to heal the soul and find true happiness.

CONTENTS

HAPPINESS

AN

INVITATION

TO

WANDER

I wish you well on this wandering path, because I am excited for the road that lies ahead of you in the pages that will unfold.

As you begin all I ask is that you go forth gently, do not rush to make your way to the end as there is nothing gained by arriving so quickly. And within the book, you may find many things that inspire your way, and if you are here to fold paper, I will share with you the techniques to folding your first paper crane.

But do not stop there, as there is much more to discover if you are willing to wander further, and throughout the book you will find many short stories and gentle wisdoms to encourage you along the path to a meaningful life. This is the journey of one thousand steps to happiness. There are also many beautiful illustrations you will find amongst the pages of the book, each one hand painted by my dear friend Niki, her beautiful brush strokes a gift to help inspire the words of each gentle wisdom within. As you find them hidden throughout the pages, take a moment to pause and appreciate when you are there, notice what you notice and feel what you feel, this too is an important part of this mindful practice.

If you have the time, I would invite you to start here and read on, each chapter is purposeful and if read in its entirety the journey can be powerful. But if you would prefer to wander a different way, simply open to any page, and wherever you are, there you will be.

I would also ask that you do not treat this book as sacred, it is not meant to be left unscathed; open it, feel the pages, the texture of the paper is dense and purposeful so do not be shy to fold the corners either. A book is meant to be a meaningful conversation, so do not hesitate to mark the pages so that you may remember them for later.

When writing this book it was important for me to share this beautiful practice. One that has inspired my life and wellbeing. Know that the stories within are my own, the way that these traditions were passed down to me, and what I have learned along my way. And while these stories are mine, the practice of folding paper belongs to us all.

And I would also like you to know that this book is for everyone, whether you are eight or eighty-eight, young in age or young at heart. I would encourage you to read together and enjoy it with others, either out loud or in quiet company, and when you are finished perhaps pass it along so that this conversation may grow, for there is so much joy to be found when we can share the practice of folding paper together.

But if you would rather read alone, know that this too is a beautiful path, one that will unfold in time, and I am here if you need me, but I am sure you will find your way.

Never rush an act
of kindness, time
plays its part

ANYTHING IS POSSIBLE

It was perfectly quiet when Koa stepped out of the house. It was very early, so the street lamps that stood guard outside her home were still wide awake, smiling and chatting away with the others that lined the street. 'Good morning, Miss Koa,' they said as she passed them by, each one bowing deeply as she made her way towards the end of the road. 'Good morning to you too, sir,' she whispered back as she scurried up the hill.

It was Monday, visiting day, and each week she would wake long before the rising sun and head to the hospital to visit her grandfather, who had been a guest there for some time now. Koa was only eight years old, but she would make this trip alone, as her parents worked long hours and so in the mornings they would sleep in until after sunrise before heading back to the factories. Her brother, Bailey, was too young to make the trip, so he, too, stayed behind.

As she started her journey towards the train station at the top of the hill, a trip she had taken many times before, she began to pick up her pace; the train left at 4.55 each morning and she knew she wouldn't make it if she didn't hurry.

'I can't miss the boarding call,' she whispered to herself as she hurried along. If only she had left the house just two minutes earlier, she would not be in such a predicament. She would later scold herself for her inefficiency. She reached into her pocket and pulled out her phone to check she had already paid for her ticket. Not doing so had caused delays in the past, and proper etiquette, as they were taught in school, was to 'always be prepared for what's next'.

But then she remembered something her grandfather used to say when they went for their 'you and me' walks – 'yumi', as he would call them. During these wanders, Grandfather would walk painfully slowly, stopping many times to look up at the sky, for he enjoyed watching the wandering clouds. He would say, 'Clouds never rush, yet they always arrive, so why should we?' Koa did not agree with many of his funny sayings; she thought they were fantasies of his aging mind. But she missed these moments dearly, and remembered them fondly.

In reality, it did not matter if she missed the first train, since a second one would be along a few minutes later and both stopped just outside the hospital, so either would get her to her destination on time. But for Koa, that was not the point: efficiency was everything. Visiting hours began at 7 a.m., and Koa prided herself on always being the first one through the door. Other visitors who knew her would often let her pass to the front of the queue, if only to help appease her ambitious mind.

As she reached the station, the train was waiting on the platform. It had stayed a few moments longer today to ensure she was on board. It was kindness like this that helped to soothe her anxious soul and made the journey ahead easier to manage. As she climbed the last stair on to the platform clearing she took a moment to zip her jacket up tight; the windows on the train had lots of cracks in them, so a chilly draught would often blow through the carriage. It took two hours and two minutes exactly to get into town and, during this time, she would look out of the window as the world sped by: a litany of cement monoliths and towering ascents dwarfed the hustling ants that scurried below. She very much enjoyed this time on the train, and some days she secretly wished the ride would never end; it was the fastest she had ever gone in her life and she knew that someday soon, when Grandfather returned home, she would no longer have these adventures.

Trains were an icon of efficiency, and everything these days ran digitally, so there was no possibility of human error. This was a rule that had been put in place long before she was born to ensure that the pleasantries of the past did not interfere with the progress of the future. Childhood was not seen as a time for fantasy or frivolity, it was an organized sequence of efficient preparations and life was a regimented schedule of advancement and technology. Anything that was deemed inefficient had been relegated to the past: gardens, playgrounds, paperback books, knitting and pop music. These and many other things were no longer tolerated. It was mandated that any activity that was undertaken for sentiment or nostalgia, or to create pleasure, rather than for ambitious outcomes, be forgotten. Everything valuable could be simulated, digitized, converted into electronic proficiencies; anything else was no longer needed. The only priority in life was ensuring success, so antiquities were replaced with phones, fast trains, talking tablets and virtual reality. Life called for efficiency over experience. Hope, too, had become a relic of the past, the wishful perspective of a bygone era.

'Beep beep beep. You are now arriving at City Centre,' the familiar automated voice murmured across the PA as the train slowed to a halt. 'Have a nice day, Miss Koa,' said the sliding doors as they disappeared into the creviced abyss between the quietude and the outside world. 'Thank you, Max. Thank you, Mimi,' she managed to say as they curtseyed away. She stood up, straightened her dress and stepped on to the platform. Reality came rushing back and swallowed her.

She checked her watch: 6.57 a.m. – she would make it on time. She emerged into the sea of swarming commuters and rode the current out on to the street before finding her way to the hospital doors. Tick . . . tick . . . tick. Seven o'clock exactly. She entered through the hospital doors. 'First, as usual. Well done, Miss Koa,' said the digital clock at the reception desk. She had arrived.

She passed through the lobby, and made her way down the hall to the lift. Once in it, she selected the floor, and the elevator began its ascent. Eight floors later, the doors opened and she stepped out into the recovery wing. The air in the hospital was always palpable, dense with the memories of the past. She arrived at Room 409. The door was closed, but through the small vertical window cut out of the door she could see that her grandfather was awake and eagerly awaiting her arrival.

'Hello, Grandfather,' she said.

Grandfather smiled warmly; he was full of spirit, though breathless and frail. 'Hello, my sweet Koa. You are as beautiful as the sun is warm. The lights have brightened now that you are here, and my heart is full, seeing you now with my aging eyes.'

To Koa, Grandfather was often long-winded and embarrassing in his compliments; he would speak in sentences instead of words, an inefficiency of old age. But she loved him so dearly.

He spoke again. 'Thank you for coming to visit me today. I have waited all week to see you and have had so much hope that you would come today so we could spend some time together.'

'Why would you need to have hope, Grandfather? It is Monday. I am always here on Mondays – why would I not be here today?' Koa replied.

Grandfather smiled knowingly. He had been in this bed for many sunsets now, and had seen many more in his lifetime. He had watched as the world hardened its grip over his children's and his grandchildren's futures, convincing them that life was measured in action and accomplishments, an evolution of misguided success. His aging soul was different and, like many misguided people of his generation, he had fought valiantly against the rising tides of change.

'May I ask you a question, Koa?' he said.

'Of course, Grandfather,' she replied.

'What do you know about paper?' he asked.

She quickly responded, 'I know many things about paper. I have read many books in the digital library at school and I saw a photo of an old paper scroll at the museum when we visited last year.' Without stopping for breath, she went on: 'In the old days, you would use paper to send messages to other people, like how we send messages today through our phones, just a lot more slowly.' She laughed. 'And books would tell stories of the past, both in truth and fiction. Paper itself was also used as a form of money so you could trade for things you wanted to buy, like food or toys.'

She paused, looking back at her grandfather to see if she had answered his questions adequately. 'But paper seems so inefficient, I am glad we have moved past those archaic times,' she added.

Grandfather smiled again, then leaned in and whispered, 'But how does paper make you feel?'

There was a long pause.

'I don't understand the question,' Koa replied.

Grandfather very gingerly reached over to his side table next to his bed, his clothes rustling as he did so. It was messy, cluttered with ornaments, his reading spectacles, a dozen tea bags and a bowl of colourful sweets. It was obvious that he came from a generation that cared not for organization. He slid open the drawer that hid beneath the overhanging chaos, pulled out a rectangular object and sat up to face her.

'Do you know what this is?' he asked.

Koa's eyes widened. 'It is a book!' She had never actually seen one in real life before, and a feeling of wonderment overcame her as she stepped closer. Nobody was allowed to own a real book any longer; any book that was found would be confiscated, digitized and then burned. Real books were a thing of the past and life these days was only concerned about the future.

She stood in awe: how did Grandfather have one in his possession? The risk was unfathomable. He began to turn the pages in his old, frail hands, speaking softly so as not to alert the nurses, knowing the illicitness of what he held. 'This is a book unlike any other, one I am sure you have never seen before. This book is the rarest of them all.' He beckoned her closer as he outstretched his hands and gave it to her.

With a wavering grip, she took the book in her two hands and held it tight. It was heavy, but it felt smooth and soft, and the cover was delicate and frail, faded red and tattered from old age and sunlight.

'Why is this book so rare, Grandfather? What is in it that makes it so special?' she asked.

'There is nothing inside; the pages are blank,' he said.

Koa began to fan the pages of the book: every page was untouched, empty, with no words; untarnished by the regiment of lines or stories, it was untamed and unwritten.

Koa had never seen blank paper before. So, this truly was a rarity.

She looked up. Grandfather's face had softened, his weary eyes were droopy and held open only by his spirited tenacity. 'I want you to have this, Koa. This paper is yours now.' She could see that sleep would come to him soon.

'But Grandfather, what do I do with it?'

'Anything you want, my darling. It is a gift of new beginnings.

'It is a place for your curiosities, unjudging of your imagination and wonderment. Its possibilities are endless. Remember, always, that the future is unwritten.'

He smiled gently as his eyes softened and said,

'But if we have paper, anything is possible.'

On some days, words are not
needed, appreciate the space
to see what unfolds

WHAT I LEARNED
FROM FOLDING PAPER

My mother taught me how to fold paper at a very young age. Maybe it was a way to distract the attention of a wayward child, or maybe it was a seed planted that would later blossom. As expected, at first there was anger and disappointment. I wanted so badly to be good that I rushed through the instructions, hoping to arrive successfully, but instead, even with the most dedicated attention, there were many misguided folds at the blunt fingertips of my youthful exuberance. There was no joy in these early moments; I was moving too fast and relentless with ambition.

My mother would say, 'Slow down. Don't think about where you will end up. Just focus on the fold, that is all that matters.' In time, I found my way, I built resilience in defeat, and learned to let go of perfection.

When folding paper, I have also learned not to expect a certain result. Many times, still when I am folding – the corners are creased or the edges blunted – and other times, a beautiful crane is created, but I have learned, no matter the outcome, it is the time that should be appreciated most, not the outcome, each moment needs only to be experienced gently.

This practice is a journey of exploration, a continuous path of gracious refinement, trying many things and judging very little. We must remember to be guided by our curiosity and be brave enough to take many steps, no matter how far we may be led astray. Life, like folding paper, is a journey of small steps and many steps, so take the time to let it unfold gently, whatever shape it may take.

Throughout my life, I have always been fascinated by how busy life has become, and I have wondered intently why humans are enamoured by immediacy and the need for instant gratification. Every day in our lives, we are tempted by life's urgency and disparity, but perhaps we are simply just moving too fast, in search of an experience that in fact requires a gentler pace? I have asked myself many times, what if we were to slow down, what would be lost? Or maybe, what would be gained? Perhaps, in a meaningful way, we can set ourselves on a new path that will unfold gently, one step at a time.

This is the practice of mindfulness. This is the gift of folding paper.

So let me invite you on a gentle wander as we heal the soul and redefine our path to happiness. This book is a mindful practice, so I invite you to read it slowly. Do not rush. Take your time to enjoy every page. There is a lot here you can explore; this is what we discover when we slow down.

These days, in my life, I tend to walk gently and spend my time enjoying the seemingly mundane, and staring out the window has become a pleasant pastime for me. Lately, I have come to enjoy exploring the corners of my own curiosity, even if it takes longer than expected; this has become a great source of joy. Sometimes people will comment with criticism, other times people may say more complimentary things, but either way I am unaffected, as this is my path, and I am happy to do so at my own pace. I have learned that speed and progress do not go hand in hand, even though we are constantly tempted by urgency in our lives.

When I was younger, stillness was not a pleasure, but instead seen as punishment, however as I've got older I have been gifted longer moments of solitude and silence, I have found many practices that have guided me into a quieter life, and time itself has been my greatest teacher. I've learned since then, though, that success is merely a subjective opinion and that happiness is not defined by accomplishments but rather by experiences.

As a meditation teacher, people often ask me if this way of life is a by-product of my meditation practice, and for the most part the answer is yes, or at least I would hope so. Meditation and other contemplative practices have helped me to ease the sharp edges of life, but I am no different to you or anyone else, I have simply learned how to slow down and prioritize my peace.

These days, I am inspired by the fact that more people are choosing to find quieter practices and calmer moments in their lives. It is only with genuine inquiry that books like these even make it out into the world. It was not long ago that the world perhaps was not ready to sit down and be quiet. In 2016, I founded Just Breathe, a mindfulness and meditation community that celebrates quieter conversations and real human connection. It started first in London and over the years has expanded globally, with thousands of people coming together for gatherings, events and quieter moments to dive deeper into the human experience. It has been a joy to see our conversation grow and I believe a gentle revolution is happening on a greater scale, now more than ever.

Throughout these events, and over the years, I have become accustomed to welcoming guests into the space by inviting them to fold paper cranes. This practice has always brought me such pleasure and presence, and so it is a tradition that I am humbled to share. When new people join us at events for the first time they are often perplexed: how is folding a paper crane a mindful practice? Is it not simply a children's activity to pass the time? My answer is always the same: 'Please, just try, and see what unfolds.'

Watching people attempt to fold for the first time has always brought me great joy, as slowly and steadily each sceptic begins to soften as they understand that their full attention is required. This is the gift of this mindful practice: letting go of our expectations and just being in the moment. Remember: attention and success are not equal endeavours.

Throughout the pages of this book, I will share with you the art of folding paper and of Senbazuru, the tradition of one thousand paper cranes (Sen = one thousand; orizuru = paper crane). In the tradition of folding one thousand paper cranes, it is said that we learn as much about ourselves as we do about folding paper, and together have a way of inspiring our path to a fulfilled life.

Now, some may have folded paper before, and if this is you, I am excited for you to read on, because you already know the power of this practice. For others, you may have tried once before, perhaps when you were younger or at school, so I hope that this may be a nostalgic reconnection and inspire you to fold once again. I also hope that, for some people, this is something new, as the joy of new beginnings is a special place to begin.

For me, I've always found this practice to be calming. These little, delicate creatures embody the human spirit; they are beautiful yet complex, vulnerable yet resilient, and when folded together in the practice of Senbazuru, they remind us just how powerful we are together.

Today, more than ever in a noisy world, I am a believer that we must have practical applications for our mindful practices. The world is moving too fast to simply try and convince people with words alone, and meditation can only do so much. As a teacher, folding paper cranes has become a valuable practice for me to share, one that guides an immediate experience in a meaningful way. Eye contact and skilful listening are two other techniques that also work remarkably well. And so, it has brought us here, with the arrival of this book, a mindful practice to teach you how to fold paper, and with it a collection of gentle wisdoms to help guide you towards a kinder way of living.

In an impatient world obsessed with quick fixes and instant gratification, let this practice be a radical perspective to slow down and go forth gently. Happiness is not a destination to achieve overnight, instead we must simply go tenderly, with hopeful intentions. It is important to know that Senbazuru is not a book of secrets, but instead a simple reminder that life is but a gentle wander of many meaningful steps, each one as important as the one before.

Ahead you will find twelve chapters, one for each step of folding a paper crane and a moment to collect along the way. My first hope is that you learn how to fold and cultivate your own practice in the art of Senbazuru. I will share with you what I have learned about this practice.

The book itself is divided into three sections, each with its own purposeful intention, and when combined they will guide you onwards and inwards. The first section is about hope, universal truths we can learn when looking to the future, and some gentle reminders that positive change is possible if you have belief and a willingness to approach with kindness. The second section is about healing, a path to return home for those who may have lost their way. If we are suffering, we must learn to come back to the present and move away from the temptations and traumas that keep us in the past. The third section of the book is about happiness, a sentiment we spend so much of our lives chasing, instead of simply living it. Let this be a perspective that helps you find your way. Remember that life is best enjoyed with small steps along the way.

As you read on, you will see that I have written many short proverbs, and these are the gentle wisdoms that are most important to remember. Return to them often and fondly, or perhaps at times when you have a wavering moment of doubt or sadness. I hope you find comfort in these words.

If the ambition is to arrive,
you will never know the
beauty of arriving

A MINDFUL PRACTICE

I would prescribe this practice for anyone who is interested, and looking for a meaningful way to slow down. I have found that these five simple principles are helpful to remember as you begin. I share them with you in hopes that they serve you well, too.

Create the Space to Fold – When beginning to fold, do not sit amongst the clutter of your day, or rush to begin with hasty actions. Take a moment to create some space in preparation, both physically and mentally. Find a clear surface that you can work on and ensure there is nothing in front of you that may get in the way or, worse, distract your attention. Things like water, food crumbs or a dirty surface may damage your paper, so take the time to clear the space and do not rush the moment. I would also encourage you not to have your phone nearby, as often its presence alone is temptation enough to distract you from your practice.

Before you begin, perhaps take a moment to sit quietly and pause. This is particularly helpful if you've had a busy day or are feeling stressed or anxious. If you practise meditation, a moment of stillness right now may serve you well too. I have found in my own experience that folding when upset or under pressure will likely create more frustration rather than less, so take your time to arrive; there is no rush to begin. On some days, however, folding paper is a good way to calm down or de-stress, as it can be helpful to give yourself just one thing to do, especially in moments when your mind is busy and your attention is struggling. In moments like this, let it be a practice of ease-fulness, not expectation.

Use a Delicate Touch – You will come to hear me say that gentleness is a necessary quality in our lives, especially now, more than ever. When we begin to fold paper, it is not the strength of our will or the force of our fingertips that serve our success, but rather our delicate touch. When handling people or stressful situations in your life, treat it, or them, with the utmost respect and with a gentle touch. When folding paper, do the same.

One Fold at a Time – In our haste for complexity, we can easily be tempted to move too fast and look beyond the present moment. We must remind ourselves often to slow down and appreciate one fold at a time.

Commit to Your Actions – There is a certain simplicity when you commit to your actions, and in the case of folding paper, this is the moment when you take action. Commitment first happens in the mind, and then follows in the fingers. I find that when folding paper, it is important to commit to your choices, so if you are folding one crane, let it be a dedicated commitment, and if you have chosen to fold one thousand cranes, do your best to complete this task and do not waver either from this commitment. As you embark on the first paper crane, simply focus on each fold in front of you and do not dwell on misguided folds along the way. In time, your dedication will always be rewarded with joy.

Celebrate What Unfolds – Do not be so bold as to think you can predict the future of this or any endeavour. Nor should you feel disappointed if what you create does not match your expectation. This is of course easier said than done. Instead, celebrate what unfolds each step of the way and find joy in your experiences. So often in life, we can become attached to what we think should or could happen, instead of what is happening, and we miss the moment as it unfolds. As you fold, do not waste time looking to the future, simply enjoy each step along the way and remember that speed plays no part in the journey. This has been the greatest lesson for me in life and in folding paper.

GETTING STARTED

Set Your Path

Take a moment to visualize the path ahead and the delicate shape of a paper crane. If this is your first time folding, do not rush yourself to begin. If you have folded many cranes before, do not bring the past into this moment. When you are ready, it is time to commit. Be here completely, give yourself the gift of this practice.

Select Your Paper

As you begin, any paper will do – a piece of newspaper, the pages of a notebook or letters that you no longer need. The beauty of folding paper is that it is an art form welcoming of all and accessible to everyone, no matter your circumstances. Know that there is no privilege when folding paper. All that is required is that your paper is square, with four equal sides. If you are using paper that is not this shape, it is best to measure and cut your paper before you begin.

However, if you are interested in knowing more, traditional folding paper, or *kami*, as it is called in Japanese, is delicate but resilient, and it is used in the practice of origami. *Ori* means 'folding' and *kami* means 'paper' (*kami* becomes *gami* when conjugated). Paper comes in all sizes, so do not be fooled into thinking there is a perfect shape. Remember that this practice is an art, not a science.

These days, *kami* is easy to find; there are many bricks-and-mortar shops and online stores that stock a wide selection. My advice is to try many types and sizes until you find the type you enjoy using most.

When selecting the thickness of paper, a lightweight and nimble paper is preferable. A thick and textured paper may feel nice to touch, but it will be more difficult to make clean folds. My preferred thickness is about 25gsm (grams per square metre), so significantly thinner than, say, paper you would put in a printer, which is usually around 80gsm. I prefer this weight because it gives both clean folds and sharp edges.

Choose the Colour

When selecting the colour of your paper, there are two ways to approach: the traditional way or your own way, and both are meaningful choices. Traditionally, in Japan, colours represent the emotion of our lives, thus each colour represents a feeling or quality that becomes empowered within and upon the wings of each bird.

Traditional Colours and Their Meanings

Deep red Inner strength and beauty, a commitment to our resilience. A connection without words.

Red Symbolizes a deep desire and passionate love.

Pink Friendship, tenderness and happiness, the colour that gifts a sense of belonging.

Orange Represents energy and enthusiasm, used to portray a zest for life and discovery.

Yellow Sunshine, a sense of freedom and joy and the promise of a sunrise, the colour of new beginnings.

Gold Symbolizes eternal loyalty and honourable actions, it is the colour of longevity.

Green Symbolizes healing, being offered a chance to grow like a flower in a garden.

Blue Stands for trust and honourable faith, a connection to our spirituality, it is the colour of hope.

Purple Represents nobility and tradition, and the importance of respectfulness.

Black Represents stability, strong roots and foundations and a feeling of empowerment.

Silver Elegance and things to be treasured.

White Innocence and purity, a need for simplicity.

Another way to select your paper is simply to choose colours you enjoy, and this, too, is meaningful. It is likely you have certain colours that have a personal meaning to you, and if so, let this inspire your choice. Sometimes, I'll fold with blue paper because it is my niece's favourite colour; other days, I'll choose green, because it reminds me of nature, the green grass and the trees. On days or occasions when you prefer to choose according to your own preferences, I encourage you to do so. Never feel the burden of tradition when crafting such a simple pleasure.

Sometimes, when we have too many choices to make, it can feel overwhelming and complicated, and by introducing the traditions and inspirations of colours my aim is not to create additional labour. Not every single crane must carry grand significance: sometimes, less is more. Sometimes I simply enjoy folding with whatever paper I can find. Do not burden yourself with grandeur in times when anything will do. The practice is in the folds, not in the shade.

Pick a Pattern

In Japan, *chiyogama* is the word used to describe repetitive patterns and designs. Patterns are often found in select types of papers and styles. Many have a cultural or ancestral inspiration. I have seen many beautiful designs in my time folding paper. In Japanese traditions, there are some patterns that have a meaningful story or influence, for example some depict the waves of the ocean or the vibrant patterns found on a kimono. Some tell the stories of a family and signify the history and heritage of the past. Often, patterns invite a specific narrative or inspiration that can give each crane a certain intentionality. Choose purposefully, if that inspires your practice.

Traditional Patterns and Their Meanings

Seigaiha – *Ebb and flow*

Kikkou – *Longevity*

Yagasuri – *Determination*

Shippo – *Harmony and peace*

Kiku – *Rejuvenation*

Asanoha – *Good health*

Finger-folding Techniques

There are many different techniques for folding paper, but I will share with you the way it was taught to me, with a three-finger fold: the thumb, index and middle finger. Folding with these three fingers allows you the evenness to control each fold intentionally.

The Anchor – One finger must always be the anchor, creating stability and certainty before any fold is made. An anchor is heavy and deliberate, and is often the first step in any fold, to ensure that the paper does not move or fly away. A strong anchor is a sign of support and selflessness; it is not the finger making the fold, but instead the steadiness and assurance to let the others take the next step.

The Guide – Once the anchor is set, the other fingers are the guides. These fingers move the paper into position and towards the actual fold. These fingers must be precise, matching the corners or lining up the edges so that a sharp fold can be made. At times, this may invite a little fear or uncertainty, but this is OK, as each fold is a learning process. Know that you can take as much time as you need to feel comfortable in the sequence of these events.

Finishing The Fold – When you are ready, make the fold, but remember: there is no rush. Use the same two fingers to finish the fold, or, if needed, you may use your other fingers to help. Remember: as in life, things work better when we work together.

As a last aside, it is also important to mention that the responsibility of each finger is ever-changing and, depending on the fold, each finger will play a different part, or on some folds a finger will have multiple responsibilities. Simply take your time and allow each fold your full attention, and you will be just fine.

A Meaningful Crease

Once you have mastered the finger-folding technique, we can move on to the proper way to create a purposeful crease or fold. There are three stages to a meaningful fold: the intention, the action and the commitment, or more simply, a beginning, middle and end.

The *intention* is what we want to do and how we want to fold. This is the first step required in preparing to fold. For example, this may be step 5, where we fold the top of the 'kite' down to create a central crease so that we can then open it up into the seashell fold (for the moment, do not worry about the names of these folds. These are just examples and will be explained as you make your way through each chapter). We must have a vision of where we are going, this is the first step to creating a purposeful fold.

The next step is the *action*, an endeavour of the heart because it is a leap into the unknown. This is the step of moving the paper into position to prepare for the fold itself. Often in this step we are lining up corners or eyeing the position of a flap in a symmetrical way. As we navigate this moment, we need a clear and focused attention, but also a gentle and heartfelt touch.

The final step in any fold is the *commitment*. When I first started folding paper, I found this stage to be the scariest, because it is definite and often we do not know the success of the fold until after it has been done. There have been many moments in my life when my folds have not lined up perfectly, but even these folds are not misguided if done with your best efforts and meaningful intentions, so think positively and consider these moments of character and creativity.

I have found, for me, that when creating a proper crease, it is best to ensure first that your paper is on a hard and steady surface, because you will need to put some effort into your crease to ensure the edges are sharp and pronounced. My preference is to crease with my index finger and press firmly as I drag my finger along the fold line, but some people prefer creasing with their thumb, as it can give a heavier and more controlled fold.

Try these different techniques, or create your own, regardless, and you will find your preference, I am sure of this. Here are three techniques that help me when creating a meaningful crease:

End To End – End to end is often the easiest technique for precision. Start at one end of your fold and press firmly at the corner with one anchor finger; from there draw the line of the fold with the other hand. It is likely that the index finger will give you the most accuracy. I find that running your finger along the fold three times helps to ensure the fold is razor sharp. The first time is to commit to the fold, while the second and third are to ensure it lasts. This is great for steps when the fold is angled or asymmetrical, like step 4 in making a crane, where the points must be triangle-folded to the midline of the shape.

Inside Out – The other technique is what I call an inside-out crease. This is where you place two fingers, usually the index finger from each hand, into the centre of the fold, press firmly and then draw away from the centre along the edge of the fold until you reach the end or corner. This is great for steps when the folds are symmetrical to the shape.

Two-way Folds – For certain folds, which I call two-way folds, it will benefit you to unfold the paper after a heavy crease. These types of folds are usually intended to create a fulcrum or crease line, rather than a finished fold line. When you are creating a two-way fold, use your techniques to create the primary fold, but then flip your paper and crease the opposite side so that the paper returns to sitting flat, as it was previously.

You will find that a crease has been created but the paper will not hold the new shape. A good example of this would again be on step 5, during the triangle fold, where the crease is to create an impression line that will then be opened up to create the seashell fold that follows. You can check out this section for more detail and discussion on inverted folds.

Support Tools

One thing I learned through my own misfortunes, is not to use a heavy hand when working with paper. Whether picking up a single piece from the table, or folding a new crease, it can be tempting to do so, but often what we gain with vigour, we sacrifice in delicacy. I have damaged the wings of many cranes in haste, and I have regretted it each time. Instead, take your time to move from fold to fold and find the rhythm in your techniques. I have collected many little tricks over the years and now often use extra tools such as the end of a pencil or a chopstick to help with certain folds. I have found that these tools can be quite helpful to slide gracefully under the problematic corners or creases of the paper. Also, a heavy book is useful in helping to deepen a fold, so I will often place a folded and flattened crane under or within the pages of a book.

What we learn from folding one crane is embodied through the time of folding one thousand

Hope is a powerful thing, a belief that change is possible and that we are all deserving of it. It is also the first step on our path to healing the soul and discovering what truly makes us happy. Above all else, hope is the belief that things will get better, even if it may seem unlikely. With a hopeful spirit, you may find that your path unfolds differently from this moment forward.

Within this chapter are the first four steps along your path: gentleness, inspiration, courage and intention. These are the qualities of a hopeful spirit.

HOPE

THE POSSIBILITY OF CHANGE

GENTLENESS

PRIORITIZING KINDNESS

I have chosen to begin by speaking of gentleness. My mother always says, 'There is nothing more powerful than a gentle breeze, for it reminds us that small moments can heal the soul.' I have found that the choice to begin gently when starting something new is often disregarded, not because it lacks appreciation, but because gentleness requires significant effort in an unrelenting world.

To live gently means prioritizing kindness and compassionate behaviour over singular acts of accomplishment. Life has a way of moving us along, nurturing our tenacity and encouraging us to move faster. And so, as we begin this journey together, choose to go slowly and take your time. Know that it is far too early to know where this will end. Do not let your expectations steal this new beginning. It is far too precious for you not to be here, now, completely.

START WITH A SINGLE FOLD

When I was a young boy, perhaps only four or five at the time, my brother would come home each day from school and sit at the kitchen table to do his homework assignments while my mother made us an afternoon snack. At the time, I was still too young to go to school but I would join him every day as he would sit to do his homework, pretending to do my own even though I had none. Each day, he would have three assignments to complete; some maths equations to solve, a handwriting practice, and a chapter of reading from whatever book had been assigned that week.

My mother always encouraged a good work ethic and so we would not be able to leave the table to go play until all his assignments were completed. On most days, it would take him about forty-five minutes to complete and then we would be free to go and play together until it was supper time. But on one such day, it did not go as planned and we were there at the kitchen table for much longer. It had been more than two hours already and he was nowhere closer to completion, he had become angry and frustrated, tears rolling down his face, his eyes swollen from the heartache.

My mother asked, 'My darling, why are you sad today? What is the reason for your troubles?'

He sobbed, 'I have tried some maths and it is too hard today, I cannot solve the equations.

'And I have tried my handwriting lesson, but my hands are angry from the equations I cannot solve, so my pen is not steady.

'And I have tried to read my book, but I am still frustrated at my handwriting and still angry with my maths equations, and so my eyes are teary and I cannot see the words on the page.

'I cannot do this homework, it is impossible, I am miserable and I am feeling quite sad.'

My mother could see his distress, and she moved closer to console him.

'My darling, let us just start gently and do one thing at a time, not everything all at once. Slow down, there is no rush, give your attention to just one moment completely and be present within it. Disregard the temptation to move too quickly, time is with you, as am I.'

Slowly the emotions subsided and thirty minutes later the assignments were completed. Sometimes in life all we need is a gentle reminder to slow down. This was a lesson I will never forget.

In life, when faced with the tasks of living we can easily become distraught or overwhelmed when we have too many things on our plate. It is easy to find ourselves overloaded with activities or accountabilities, or if we have agreed to attend too many events with friends or co-workers only to find we have taken on too much and feel like we have too little time. All of which can create frustrations and a feeling of being stuck. We can become anxious or grief-stricken and descend into a feeling of helplessness and uncertainty. This is the case of what happened to my brother that day at the kitchen table, and a similar case of what many people find themselves in when moving too fast and taking on too much.

But to break this cycle is not always easy, the world often rewards us for moving fast and coping with complexity. And so, we must remind ourselves often, and also each other, that to slow down and be gentle in our actions is a great act of kindness in a world that is asking otherwise. Perhaps this is the bravest act of rebellion in a busy world.

Do one thing at a time,
not everything all at once

DO NOT BE TEMPTED
BY EXPECTATION

The first time I meditated, I was fifteen years old. I was hanging out with a friend at his home and we were sitting in his living room, watching TV and talking about school that day. At the time, his grandfather was visiting. He was a Buddhist monk who lived in Japan but during the colder months of the year would visit them for a few weeks to spend time with the family.

Growing up I had spent many afternoons at my friend's house, but this was the first time I had met his grandfather. He was a gentle and soft-spoken man and you could feel the warmth of his personality long before he opened his mouth to speak. On that day, he entered the living room and sat down next to us in an armchair. He did not speak at first, he just sat and listened to us chat away about the day, happily smiling and nodding along to our conversation as if to indicate that he was listening.

I was soon introduced as a friend from school and only then did he begin to join the conversation.

I had never met a real Buddhist monk before, I had only seen them in films or read about them in books, so I was interested to know more about his life and practices. He told me that he woke up early each morning before sunrise to meditate, and then would spend the first hours of his day in silence before engaging with the world around him. His demeanour was friendly and inviting so I felt comfortable asking more questions about his life. My friend, who had heard his grandfather speak of his routine often, was not particularly interested in hearing more, so he got up and went to the kitchen to make a snack and fetch a drink of water, leaving us to continue our conversation alone.

His grandfather asked me, 'Have you ever meditated before, ?' I said no, I had never tried, but I was interested to try. He asked me if I would like to try a short practice and, naturally, I said yes.

'What will happen?' I asked.

'What do you think will happen?' he answered.

I responded, 'I am sure it will feel wonderful. I expect to feel calm and at peace.' I had heard that meditation would help to clear your mind and put you at ease, so I was certain that this, too, would be my experience.

'I know I will love it, and I know I will be good at it, too,' I said, feeling a natural calling at that moment to the practice.

'Let us begin then, and see what occurs. Please close your eyes. I will let you know when it is time to come back,' my friend's grandfather said.

For the next few minutes, I sat there, 'meditating', and it was miserable. There was no pleasure, no enjoyment, just discomfort

Letting go is a choice
for new beginnings

and boredom. Where was the bliss that I was expecting?

A few minutes later he said, 'OK, you are finished, please open your eyes.' I do not know how long I was sitting there, but it felt like an eternity.

He asked, 'How do you feel?'

I considered lying, I so badly wanted to impress him and say I enjoyed the practice. I'd had high hopes that I would be a great meditator, but I was not. But I could not lie to him, that would be dishonest, so I responded, 'It was OK, but I am not sure it is for me. I am sorry, I do not think that I am very good at meditating.'

He smiled. 'I understand,' he said. 'You think you have failed, don't you?'

Feeling frustrated and deflated, I nodded. I so badly wished I had been better.

He said, 'Do not think you have failed. The problem you are facing is that your ego desires to be successful. This is not the practice and because of it, it has caused you to miss the moment completely. Even in meditation, you are trying to succeed.'

Often in life we are quick to give permission for our desires to outweigh our experiences, and we unwillingly forfeit our present attention to the temptations of certain achievements. In this instance, my mind cared only for success, and because of this, I missed entirely the experience on offer.

Many years later, this experience has come full circle as I myself am now a meditation teacher. Often, when new students sit for the first time, they, too, are expecting a profound experience, just like I was many years ago when sitting with this Buddhist monk, and like mine, their expectations will often fall short and they will often feel their time has been wasted. On these occasions, I share with them the same story that I have shared with you now, and I remind them that a truly present experience requires a non-striving attitude. What I have learned above all else is that we must be vigilant with our attention, for it is too easy for our temptations to lead us astray.

Do not let your ambitions steal this moment, for the beauty of our presence is knowing that the ego resides outside it.

True presence
is a gift the ego
cannot steal

DO NOT RUSH
A MEANINGFUL WANDER

One of my favourite things to do when I am visiting a new city is to spend an afternoon wandering the streets without a plan or specific purpose. If I am there to teach or share a talk, I will always try to arrive a day early so that I have time to be with the city, uninterrupted. Often, I travel alone and arrive with only a bag, a small set of belongings and this beautiful gift of time. This is an essential pleasure in my life and one I will partake in as often as my schedule allows.

In preparation for these afternoons, I do not bring anything in excess, I leave books and computers in my hotel room and I do my best to minimize being on the phone or social media accounts. I make a concerted effort to enjoy the day without a set schedule and I do my best to remove regularity and habituated routines where possible. I find that during this time alone, it is necessary to have a break from familiar attachments and intentionally disrupt the addictions of predictability and be with the day completely.

These days in the habituated schedule of our lives, we simply move too fast. We shuffle from task to task, accomplishing one thing and then quickly moving on to the next. For the most part, our days are strictly regulated, with set times to wake up, to eat meals and we follow a precise schedule that helps us move through our days with an ambitious sequence. But I find that on busier days and with people with even busier lives, the time to rest and the space for a wandering mind is often disregarded or forgotten.

And so, on my travels when I have these afternoons alone and free, I am committed to inaction and thoroughly enjoy the time to be at peace. Often the effects will be immediately profound, I will become newly inspired, inspiration comes flooding in and creativity comes flowing out. My mood will elevate and my attitude will brighten, everything is exciting and every minute enjoyable. Often we must give ourselves intentional reprieve from our rigorously scheduled lives so that we will feel the benefits of doing less.

I have learned there are three things that help ease my day.

First I will remind myself I have nowhere else I need to be and there is nothing more urgent that needs my attention in this moment. I will commit to seeing everything as completely new, because familiarity can often be a great distraction because it tempts us to believe that we do not need our fullest attention.

The second is realizing that no one will miss me for just one day. Often, we can convince ourselves that we are more important than we are, and that we must be available and accessible at all times to the people in our lives. But this is not true as unfortunate as it may sound. Ask yourself this though, do you need to know the whereabouts of friends and family each and every minute of the day? Unlikely. In most cases we are OK not knowing every action or occurence of their day. And so, do not let your mind convince you that you are always needed to be accounted for, and when we become comfortable knowing that for a day it is OK to be forgettable, we in turn become free and the burden of expectation subsides.

The third thing is reframing the idea that a day to yourself is not a 'day off' from life, but instead a day that is truly turned on to it. When we are undisturbed by the conversations of others, or the routines of our home life, we are left with the space to reconnect and rediscover what fulfils us and brings us joy. Taking a day to yourself to be quiet and alone, will serve you well.

And so, we must all find our way towards a gentle wander, and make way for moments that break our cycles of familiar actions. For me it is travel and an aimless afternoon, for you it may be something else, like a walk in the countryside, or the confines of a good book. You may wish to sit for hours listening to the scratchy sounds of vinyl records or spend time with the strokes of your paint brush. Whatever it is, allow yourself the time to wander, to be with your thoughts and to feel what's within you. Move inwards towards uninterrupted moments and I promise you will find that these are the experiences that are both breath taking and breath making, and the ones that make life truly worth living.

Do not take my gentleness
as a lack of character, for it is
the essence of a joyful life

BEFORE YOU BEGIN

Now, before you begin folding, take a moment to lay the paper gently on the table in front of you. Pause, remove your hands, do not be so eager, we have only just begun, so take a moment to just breathe. Allow yourself the gift of arrival, close your eyes, notice how still this moment can be. What do you feel? Can you feel more? If this is your first time folding, notice if expectations are rising. If this is you, perhaps consider sitting a bit longer until these sensations calm. Ambition is not needed in this practice.

I've learned in time that the best way to start is to stop, because for any new beginnings our expectations can easily be tempted. I find that one way to do this is to start simply by becoming aware of what's in front of you: open your eyes and allow yourself to get lost in the vibrant colours and patterns before you. What is it that you see? A deep red or a warm green, a vibrant yellow or a calming blue? Gift yourself this time to appreciate all that is happening before any folds are made. There is immense beauty in the moment before the moment, but you must make the space and allow it to happen unaffected. This is the practice of mindfulness.

If this is all new for you, I must commend you already, for slowing down and doing less is a brave choice these days in a busy world, and even if it is uncomfortable, do not rush, as there is so much we can learn in allowing ourselves to simply feel what is. Try not to ruin this moment with the aspirations of your fingertips.

We must also be clear that each step requires effort. It does not need to be grand; in fact, I prefer it not to be. Effort itself is nothing more than action with intentionality, and remembering this will serve you well as things unfold. Take your time along the way, have patience and do not be so eager for immediate accomplishment. Feel no obligation to keep a certain rhythm; you can – and I encourage this – revisit any previous steps along the way until you feel comfortable enough to continue. Progress does not need to have speed or direction. As you continue, there will be times when your effort will feel confident. This is a good sign, and familiar and repetitive folds will help with this feeling, as will time and experience, so seek out these familiarities where you can, for these moments will gift you the feeling of ease.

As you make your way through the pages of this book, I will share the guidance for each step at the end of each chapter. Take your time to enjoy the stories and gentle wisdoms, and do not rush to finish your folds. One suggestion would be to use a single sheet of folding paper as your bookmark. Take it with you as you make your way throughout the journey, and as the story unfolds, your crane will begin to take shape.

STEP ONE
THE DIAGONAL FOLD

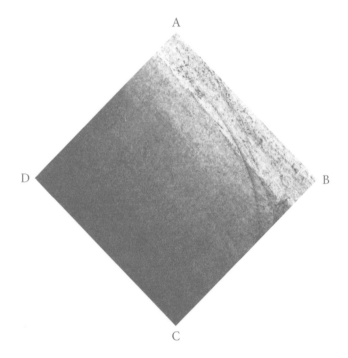

Start by folding the paper in half diagonally with the coloured side of the paper facing upwards. Fold corners A to C, undo the fold and then fold again from B to D. Steady the paper as you begin, not too tight, but firm enough so that it does not go awry. Move slowly, far more slowly than you would perhaps think, because a misstep on the first fold can cause long-lasting suffering, especially if you are new to the practice. The aim is not perfection, but instead intention, so fold delicately and meaningfully. Do not rush, but be sure.

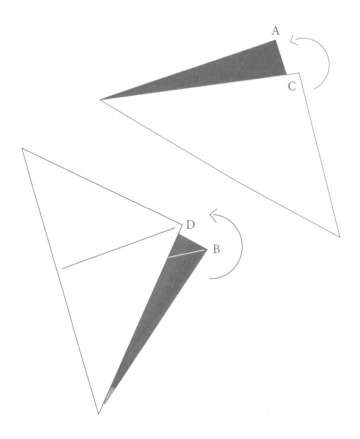

Take a moment to run your fingers along the edge of both folds, front and back, giving each one enough attention to ensure that the edges are sharp. Run your fingers along the long edge firmly, slowly and intentionally. And then unfold the paper and lay it flat on the table. You are committed, so dive in wholeheartedly. The first step is complete. It has begun. You are on your way.

COURAGE

WILLINGNESS TO TRY

In life, we may often think ourselves inadequate or not ready, and we can persuade ourselves to believe that we are incapable of progress because the tasks ahead are too big or have come too soon. But a brave act is not measured in distance but rather in intention, and courage is simply having the willingness to try.

When people think of courage, it is easy to say, 'I am not brave so I cannot be a courageous person.' Often, in life, we see brave heroes who, in the face of danger, fight fearlessly to save the world from harm or heartbreak, and we have become accustomed to these triumphs being the benchmark of how courage is defined. But there are also many courageous acts that may be far less grandiose in their execution but may be equally as profound in their meaning. Many of our greatest acts of bravery are often done in small and quiet steps.

Courage is a willingness to step into the unknown, a practice of our vulnerabilities in action.

In life, we may choose any path
to walk, but we must choose

THE FOUR PATHS

When walking along a trail, if you come to an intersection where the road splits, it is common to stop and consider which way is best to go. Often, if the divide is unanticipated, we can become unsure of the best direction to choose, and become overwhelmed by indecision. We look to all our options to figure out which is our best path and try to predict the road ahead.

But imagine, at this crossroads, there is a man waiting for you as you arrive, and you ask him, 'Which way shall I go? There are too many paths to choose.'

He says, 'If you go left, the road is rocky and dangerous, and you may fall to your death!'

'So, I should not go left, I do not want to die, I should go right instead,' you say.

'But if you go to the right, there are snakes, and you will get eaten alive,' he replies.

'So, I should not go right, I do not want to get attacked by snakes, I will continue on the path ahead,' you say in response.

'But if you stay on this same path, there is a tall mountain to climb, and you may not be strong enough to conquer it and you will lose the heart to go on,' he says assuredly.

'So, I should not go ahead. I am not sure I will have the strength. Perhaps I should turn around and return home.'

'But you cannot turn around. Your family will think you are a failure and you will bring great shame to your parents,' he says.

'So, what shall I do? I have no path to walk.'

Often, when we are faced with our doubts, we find ourselves at the intersection of this same uncertainty and we feel unable to move in any direction because all roads lead to defeated outcomes. But this is not true: it is simply our mind believing in the delusion of our doubts by all forseeable outcomes.

To be brave is not to be in the absence of doubts but to understand them and realize how they can limit us from taking meaningful action. The man in the story is the voice in our heads, convincing us that any outcome will lead us to misery.

And so, I have come to speak of our doubts in four different ways, like the four paths at the crossroads, and in understanding each one, we can learn how we can find our way.

The first path is fear, the path of the dangerous road. Fear is a projection of a failed future and the anticipation that something will go terribly wrong. In our minds, we are convinced that a dangerous path will lead to certain death, and whatever could go wrong, will go wrong, and so this path is not an option worth choosing. But fears are like fortunes, and are not rooted in truth, it is simply our mind in a downward spiral towards negativity and catastrophe. And so, if we choose this path, we should not fear disaster, we must simply walk with care knowing that fear is simply our misguided imagination.

The second path is overthinking, the path of the snakes. Overthinking is the turmoil of our paradoxical mind, and we can easily convince ourselves that the snakes are unfriendly and unkind. What if they are sleeping and do not want to be disturbed? But, on the other hand, what if they are not and would welcome our friendly visit? But what if they are? But what if they are not? And so we spin in circles and the cycle repeats, never knowing, never going anywhere. Our doubts have a way of creating adversity in times when we are unsure, and this will cause us to unravel and churn, a perpetual cycle for an eventual disaster that may never come. In times of overthinking we must break this pattern, since a worried mind will never move forward and we will never truly know if the road ahead will lead to friend or foe.

The third path is uncertainty, the path of the mountain. Uncertainty is an emotion of the soul that can cause deep heartache. As humans, we can often lack self-confidence and self-belief, and we can feel a need for constant validation and emotional assurance. We look to our friends and the people closest to us to remind us that we are deserving and capable. Life has a way of convincing us we are unworthy or incapable, and so we must nurture strong connections with others and share kind words whenever possible, especially to ourselves. All acts of love are supportive, and even if you may think your kindness small, know there is no measure of love that is unappreciated in the heart. Love and self-belief are the resolution to uncertainty.

The final path is regret, the path behind us we've not yet left behind. Regret is the residue of negativity of our past experiences, but we must come to learn there is no shame in your shadows. Own them; they are part of the journey that has brought you here. When standing at the crossroads of doubt and indecision, know you can always go back if it helps you move onwards, going home is always an option: there is no failure in returning to the people who love you.

And so, these are the four paths we face, or as I like to call them, the F.O.U.R. paths of doubts – fear, overthinking, uncertainty and regret – each with its own negative narrative to distract us from our way. But knowing this we must stand bravely at the crossroads of our insecurities and choose to rise above our doubtful distractions and move forward no matter which direction you choose.

Fear is the result of
wasted expectation

It is not the mountain
that needs to bend, but
you who needs to rise

DO NOT BLAME
THE MOUNTAIN

The mountain cares not if you begin,
It is not the enemy you desire,
The mountain does not have an opinion,
It cares not if you retire.

The mountain is a mountain,
It does not stand in your way,
So do not blame the mountain,
For it is you that must rise today.

THE TRUTH OF
THE TURTLE

When you think of courageous animals, it is not likely that you will first think of the turtle. Perhaps you might think of the hippopotamus, or a rhinoceros, or maybe a brave sparrowhawk, but the turtle – it is unlikely.

Often when we speak of courage, we can be fooled into believing that courage and might are the same, but they are not. For example, it is easy for a gorilla to pound its chest in a jungle full of animals that already bow to him, or an eagle to soar in revelry above his prey, which already fears him, but this is not courage, it is simply the actions of their given nature and their place within the kingdom.

But the turtle is not known for its bravery, it is quiet and timid and at the first sign of danger hides away in its shell, protected so the world cannot hurt it when it is safely inside. But the turtle knows that there is no progress when it is hidden away, it cannot move forward, so in time it must re-emerge, in the face of danger or whatever lies waiting outside.

The courage of a turtle is not in its retreat but in the decision to step back into the light.

The true courage of the turtle is knowing that it must stick its neck out in order to once again move forward. Growing up I have always loved this story of the turtle. It was first told to me by my father when I was a young boy.

Looking back it always reminds me that as humans, we are very much the same as the turtle. When we feel threatened, we can hide, we shrink, we move inside; it is the natural action of preservation. But we must also realize that this is not a place to reside for ever, and so we, too, must muster the courage to re-emerge, vulnerably but willingly.

We must always remember that our progress is not a measure of effort but of intention.

In times of uncertainty, be the turtle.

Never measure the
first step in distance

STEP TWO
THE BOOK FOLD

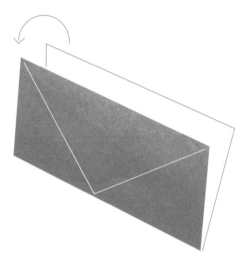

Turn the paper over so that the coloured side is now facing down. The next step is what I call a book fold, folding the left-hand side of the paper over to the right, like a curling wave crashing into the sea. Start by placing your middle finger on the right-hand side of the paper in the centre of the long edge: this will be your anchor, a single point of steadiness that creates the foundation of the fold. From there, use your left hand to gently guide the fold and build the swell of the paper wave. Lift the left edge up and over to create a beautiful arc as it moves to align with the right edge. This is an action that requires a delicate touch. My mother used to say, 'Measure twice, cut once.' I like to think that this applies well to this fold. It is here that I prefer to flatten the folded paper by pressing and drawing a firm line from the anchor to the centre of the adjacent paper wave. For this step, I prefer to crease my folds from the inside out, using the index finger of

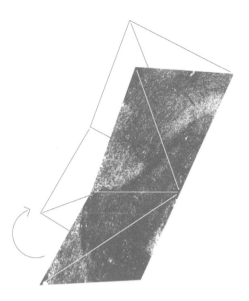

both hands to draw outwards along the fold line. Because of its rising tide, I must admit that at times this fold can be daunting, but do not make more of the moment than it needs to be: go slowly and you will be just fine. For me, I enjoy sealing the fate of each fold, and now that you have completed the first book fold, we must prepare for the second. The second book fold is the same as the first; turn the paper ninety degrees and fold again. This second fold will be easier than the first. This is the benefit of repetition and familiarity. After you complete the second fold, reopen the paper and return the sheet to the original square shape and how it was when you began. The coloured side of the paper should again be face down. Now lie it flat and smooth it out once with your fingers. The paper now carries the wrinkles of time and the first few footsteps of your folds. This is a beautiful moment to enjoy. Again, don't rush.

INSPIRATION

A SPARK OF POSSIBILITY

As humans, we are naturally creative beings, always curious about the wonderments of life, exploring the line between what is real and what is possible, but often we can feel uninspired and unimaginative in a world that demands efficiency over creativity.

If we are moving too fast or are stressed by the speed of life, then inspiration may be fleeting. When times are tough, or our attentions distracted, inspiration retreats. In cultivating hope, we must unburden ourselves of the past and see only the possibilities that lie ahead. Slow down and inspiration will spark. Be ready to receive it, because, once captured, the world will ignite and anything is possible.

Beyond the horizons,
all life must be created

A SINGLE SPARK
LIGHTS ALL FIRES

If you have ever struck a match, you know that it takes nothing more than a spark to start a fire; in one flick of the wrist, light and life are created. And this, too, is the experience of inspiration: a single spark can change everything. On many occasions in my life, I have been struck by inspiration in times and places when I was not expecting it. I remember once when I was teaching a meditation course to a group of students and a question was asked about the best time of the day to meditate. As I began to answer, I looked around the room and noticed that two students had the same exact pair of socks on. It was, of course, not relevant to the discussion, but nevertheless caught my eye.

The socks were light blue, similar to the colour of the sky on an autumn afternoon when the air is crisp and you can see your breath with every exhalation, and on them were an array of little white polka dots lined up perfectly in organized rows, each about the size of a small pebble. It was fascinating to me that in a small room of only a few students, two people had arrived wearing exactly the same socks. I was amazed.

But as I was still teaching, I could not let this observation steal my focus completely, and so I set my curiosity aside and returned to the original question being asked. But throughout the rest of the lecture I could not help but find myself glancing back at the socks periodically. I was captivated, noticing intently the patterns and vibrancy of the colours. They had caught my attention and had ignited my inspiration.

Now you may wonder why I was so entranced with these socks. What did they inspire within me? Well, coincidentally, the week before I had moved into a new home and had been searching for inspiration on how to paint one of the walls in the house. I had spent many hours that week looking through magazines and art books in search of the right colour and patterns to brighten the space. And, in this moment, I found what I had been looking for.

The beauty of inspiration is that it is not a linear process. We cannot simply choose to be inspired or imaginative at prescribed times; it is something that can happen whimsically and when we are least expecting it, much like me in this moment with these blue socks. But what is important to recognize is that inspiration is a gift, and when it does come is struck like a match, that creates something we have not yet imagined before. Inspiration is an opportunity to go beyond what we already know and discover the possibility of something new.

At sunrise, the first spark of
light is the most curious

EVERYTHING FIRST
MUST BE IMAGINED

If I am not here,
Look beyond the horizon.
There you will find me.

What you do not know
is not unknown

MAKE SPACE TO RECEIVE

Inspiration is like a meaningful conversation: we cannot demand it or force it to happen, but when it does, it is profound. And so, we must learn to be unambitious, remembering that it is not an achievement to capture or an experience to collect. Inspiration does not abide by a schedule or follow a certain rhythm, and it cannot be found if we are moving too fast. Inspiration is the first stage of true transformation, a spark that creates endless possibility and an awareness that leads to positive change. So, we must cultivate quieter moments when we are un-striving, but knowing we must always be open to receive.

You Cannot Push Water Uphill

Inspiration is no match for urgency. If time is the priority, imagination wanes and creativity may expire. In these moments, we must resist the temptation to move faster; effort and ambition will not help you. And while time itself will not change, inspiration will continue to flow. One stone should never decide the path of the river.

A Child Who Thinks He Is Deserving Rarely Is

We must never take our inspirations for granted. Be grateful you have been given this gift of creativity. See each moment as precious whenever we are lucky enough to receive.

A Watched Kettle Never Boils

Inspiration does not appear if you are waiting for it to arrive. Instead, place your attention elsewhere so that you are ready when it does. Grant yourself time to wander, whether in footsteps or in moments of the mind. Trust that it will come, but do not worry when.

A butterfly
only lands on
quiet hands

STEP THREE
THE SANDWICH FOLD

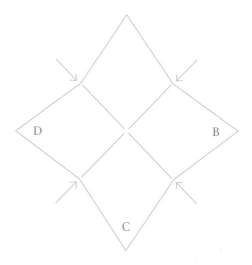

This is the first step of real transformation, but it is also a fold that can lead to frustration and confusion. Why? Because this step requires complex action, a delicate touch and an assertive vision. In front of you is a single unfolded piece of paper, the underside facing outwards, with the faint creases of the diagonal and book folds from steps 1 & 2. Take a moment to position the paper like a diamond rather than a square, as you will find it easier in this position to manoeuvre the next fold. First, gently take the outer two corners of the paper (B & D), one in each hand between the thumb and first finger, and pull them inwards towards the bottom corner (C). This will create the bottom fold of the shape, with a small section of colour or pattern now peaking upwards.

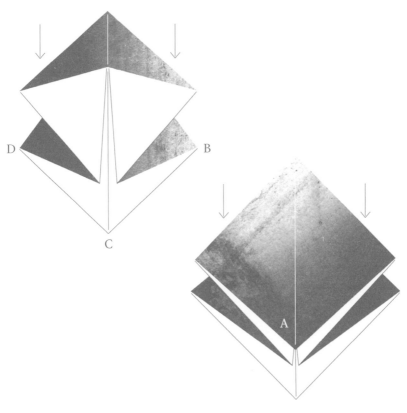

To finish the fold, press down from the top of the paper and close the cavernous space that has been created, by folding the top point (A) down to the bottom, like the lid on an open hatch. As you press down, run your fingers along all the edges of the new folded diamond shape to ensure that it sits flat, firm and in place. This fold can feel very rewarding, because we have created a new shape completely: we are in transformation.

INTENTION

COMMITMENT TO HOPE

It is important in life that hope is enduring; we cannot be hopeful only for a fleeting moment, believing that this is enough to encourage us on our onward path. And so, we must cultivate a strong resolve that guides our actions and inspires our perspective, and this is the practice of meaningful intentions.

When setting intentions, we must be clear, and dedicate our attention to these inward commitments, for it is in our hearts where our most meaningful actions start. A strong intention is the gift to explore, knowing that our path is lit with a hopeful spirit, which will guide us wherever we choose to wander.

A firm step knows its path

CHOPSTICKS OR FORKS?

Growing up, my family would eat dinner together every night, sharing a meal that my mother had made for us to enjoy. As part of the dinner ritual, my brother, sister and I would have regular duties to attend to before and after each meal. Often, when I retell this story, many people will smile and laugh, as they, too, had something similar in their household. Now, as we were three children, there were three different jobs for each meal – one person was responsible for setting the table, someone else was in charge of clearing it after the meal, and whoever was left had to do the washing up afterwards – and we would each take our turn doing each one. Even now, as adults, each with our own family, whenever we are all together, the same three tasks are expected to be done.

Thinking back to those childhood years, I remember we all had our preferences and, to this day, I am certain this is still the case. My sister, Nicole, who is the youngest, would often get first choice on what she preferred to do. She was quite a creative child – she loved her colouring books, crayons and playing with her toys – and so she was always extremely reluctant to come to dinner before she had to, as she saw it as punishment to have to stop playing before it was time to eat. This meant that, most nights, she would choose to clear the dishes and take them from the table to the kitchen sink. This was also the easiest job, so she was not shy to select this one often. My brother, Andrew, was the oldest. He was also the kindest and would often let me choose next, between setting the table and doing the dishes, and every time I would always choose the former, because setting the table meant I was also part of the cooking and preparation, which to me was more exciting than being the clean-up crew.

As a small boy, I loved being in the kitchen with my mother. She called me her little sous chef. If the eggs needed cracking, I was ready and willing; if the onions needed dicing, I would happily fight through the tears; and if the rice needed to be put on, she had trained me well. It was always my dream to become a chef.

Maybe, one day, I still will. There is always time.

When getting ready for dinner, my mother would always remind me that setting the table was a very important task. She would say, 'You cannot enjoy soup with a fork,' which meant, in setting the table for the meal ahead, a clear intention was always needed. Now, in our house, dinner came in two distinct flavours, traditional or 'other'. Traditional meant rice plus tofu, meats and vegetables, while the latter meant Western food like pasta or roast chicken and potatoes, grilled fish or green salads. And so, when it was time to set the table I would only need to ask one simple question: 'Chopsticks or forks?' And the answer would give me all I needed to know about the intentions of the meal. If my mother said, 'Chopsticks,' it meant it was likely to be served family-style, so I would need chopsticks plus rice bowls, side plates, sauce dishes and serving spoons; if she said, 'Forks,' it meant large plates, salad plates, bread basket, butter knives and sharp knives – two completely different settings for the meal that was to come. This one simple question allowed me to set the table for purpose. And with purpose and, in life, sometimes all we need is a clear intention to show us how to truly enjoy what's to come.

**We must always
set the table before
we sit down to eat**

PERFECTION IS A MYTH
WE NEED NOT CHASE

If you have ever prepared a pot of rice, you will know that perfection is both subjective and unforgiving. The preparation and timing are both an art and a skill, and it is something that can take many years to master before you could ever consider yourself capable. I believe that learning to make rice is a skill that is essential learning for both children and adults alike, not only to fill your belly but, more importantly, as a lesson in why we need not chase perfection.

Like most children, it was my mother who first taught me how, and I would imagine this is similar for you if your family had rice most evenings, like mine. What we must first know about the preparation is that it is not an exact science; rather, it is an art form learned and a skill acquired in time: your sight, your touch and the feel of the grains all play an equal part. What's more, most families will have their own recipes for preparation – some will add a pinch of salt, or a splash of rice vinegar, and I have friends who will even add a dash of sugar to sweeten, all in certain proportions – so it is impossible to agree on a perfect recipe or technique for preparation.

But no matter the process, every time is different, so do not chase perfection for it does not exist and you will never arrive.

Do not waste an arrow on a windy day

MY MOTHER'S RECIPE

When making rice, you do not need much: a pot, the grains, water and your two hands. This is the way it was taught to me and the way I will share with you now. As you begin, do not be distracted by measuring cups, the palm of your hand is all you need to measure the right amount. One cupped palm of rice per person is usually good, do not over think this step, this is usually more than enough.

The next step is to wash the rice so that the dirt and husk falls away, use gentle circles to move the grains thoroughly. Use warm water, this is to ensure that each grain begins to soften. The first time you rinse the rice, the water will be cloudy, the second time, slightly less. Keep repeating the process until the water runs clear, even if it takes more than a few times.

Now you are ready to measure the water. But how do you know what amount is enough? Let me teach you the traditional way, the way it was taught to me. The secret to measure just the right amount of water is to use your middle finger, touch the top of the rice grains and fill the water up until it reaches the first line of your fingertip.

Let me be the first to say that there is no science in this approach, only wisdom and experience, and many bowls of rice that have been made this way. You may laugh, as many do, but if you ask any mother or grandmother, this is often the way. Now you are ready to cook, cover with a lid and set it on the stove top. All that remains is time, patience and gentle heat. But know that once you begin, you are committed, nothing more can be done. Give the rice time to steam, do not stir the pot or lift the lid and the water should never boil, a simmer at most is needed. After 15 to 20 minutes the rice will be warm and inviting. And if so, it's ready.

Trust the process and let the time blossom: this is the best recipe for life, and making rice.

Do not strive for
perfection, for
it is a waste of
the imagination

COMMIT TO YOUR JOY

In times of celebration, it is customary to dance, and I have come to love occasions when I can cut loose and have fun. Now, I must say, I am not the best dancer, but this will not stop me from having a good time and enjoying the music and finding my rhythm.

And over the years, I have found that my enjoyment of dancing is twofold. The first aspect of it is simply to have fun and be in the moment, and when I am invited to a party or other celebratory occasion I will always find a way to get on the dance floor with old friends and new ones, or if no one else is interested, I am not shy to go alone. For me, it is blissfully freeing and one that brings me so much joy. Now I must say, I do not have the greatest sense of rhythm, but this is not the point; it is simply a chance to let loose and have fun. I have found that, when dancing, enjoyment can only be found if we are in the moment, unjudging and free.

The second reason I enjoy dancing is that most people do not expect me to. As a meditation teacher, people often expect me not to partake in such light-hearted activities, as perhaps they see me as a quiet and reserved person. My mannerisms are not sharp or gestured, and I rarely raise my voice or waver in tone, and so it is quite surprising for some when they see a different side of me.

Some people's opinions will quickly change, as if my choice to enjoy myself has broken the trust of our relationship. Perhaps my dancing does not align with their perception of a meditation teacher. Some will even say, 'A teacher should not act in this way.' And that is OK: their opinions are not for me to control, and nor do I care to entertain their distrust.

I have found through the experience of dancing that it is not our place to care what others think of us. People will always have opinions, but they are not my burden to carry. We must be committed in making the choices that bring us the most joy, and doing so purposefully. Whatever it is that makes you happy, find what excites you and do not waver if others think less of you for it. Commit to your joys, do not short-change your passions, and leave behind any temptations or expectations that others may try to control you with. Step firmly and dance proudly, for the commitments you keep will always lighten the load on your path towards a life of happiness and fulfilment.

A stone
has no
purpose,
until
it does

STEP FOUR
THE KITE FOLD

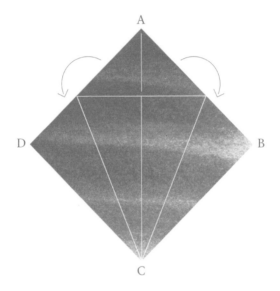

This fold is about finding intention as we move inwards, towards the centre of the shape. As we look down at the smaller diamond shape in front of us, we have transformed our single sheet of paper into a shape that has both simplicity and complexity. To make the kite fold, turn the shape clockwise a quarter turn so that the folded opening of the shape is now pointing to the left. If it is easier to follow the references to points A, B, C and D, then, at this stage, corner B is at the bottom. The reason I make this quarter turn is that I find it easier to fold upwards. Now fold the long edge between corners B and C towards the central horizon line so that the edge lines up with the middle of the shape. Corner B will now also sit along this same line. Be aware that, at this stage, you

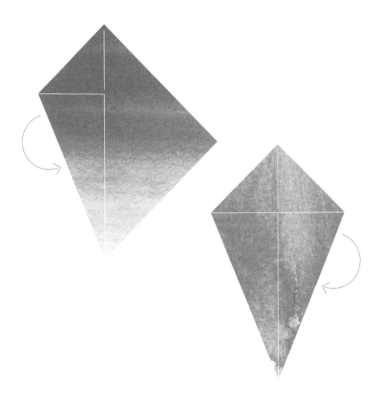

are only folding the top flap of the shape. Once it is completed and has a firm crease, draw your finger along the edge of the new fold to ensure that it is grounded and set; this edge is necessary for future folds. And then repeat this same fold with the adjacent top flap. Once you have completed the top-side flap folds, you will need to flip the crane over and fold in the corners on the bottom side. This is a practice of repetition, not perfection. Often, when folds are repeated, we are gifted the chance to make amends. If our first attempt didn't go as planned, don't dwell on it but learn from it and adjust for what comes next. You should now have a shape that we call 'the kite fold'.

At times in life, we must all heal, whether it is a broken bone or a broken heart. It is the choice to return to the present and to let go of the suffering that keeps us attached to what is behind us. But know, if you have ever experienced suffering or hardship but have not given up, then you are on a healing path. In time, all wounds will recover, so take your time, be patient and focus on new habits and perspectives to help you find your way back to this moment completely.

In this section of the book, we speak of four themes on the path to healing: forgiveness, patience, resilience and support. Each one is important on our onward way.

Holding on is a commitment to hope, but letting go is a choice for new beginnings. Both are meaningful on the path to healing.

HEALING

RETURNING TO THE PRESENT

FORGIVENESS

RELEASING ATTACHMENT

Forgiveness is an ongoing practice. If we have been ill treated by someone close to us, a partner or a friend, the suffering we feel can stay with us for a long time. Perhaps we could even believe that an apology is owed to us – but what if both people think they are right? No middle ground will be found. Nothing will happen, and the suffering will continue. A lack of forgiveness is a negative cycle of fault and frustration.

If it is our trust that has been broken, we become a person who is untrusting; if someone has stolen from us, we become doubtful of people's genuine nature. Without forgiveness, we are unable to experience life without the negative influence from our past. Without forgiveness, we can never truly be present. But once we forgive, attachments subside.

Be not the hand with the
tightest grip, but the one
with the least to hold

SUFFERING IS A CHOICE
WE NEED NOT CHOOSE

When I was in my late twenties, I attended sessions with a meditation teacher whose name I've since, sadly, forgotten. In these sessions, we would sit for hours, both in silence and in quiet conversation. One time, I remember, a woman attended who was distraught with emotions from a recent break-up with her long-term partner. She had attended these sessions before, so I recognized her face, and even though I had not spoken to her, she was familiar to me.

Every other time I had seen her she had been bright and vibrant, always chatty and brimming with confidence, but on this occasion, I remember her being quite upset and heartbroken. Throughout the session, she just sat against the wall at the back of the hall, disengaged with the conversation, weeping loudly, for all the room to hear. Now and then, someone would attempt to comfort her, but she was, in all senses, inconsolable. Up until this point, the teacher had given her no specific attention, he simply acknowledged her on arrival, as he did with all students, with a simple nod and a gesture to be seated. But because of her ongoing disruption, I, like most people, had expected him to engage in a consoling conversation. However, he did not.

For the next twenty minutes, her weeping could be heard throughout the hall, and you could see that the other students were beginning to become restless and disturbed. I thought to myself, perhaps she should excuse herself, but she carried on, and so did the group. Eventually, it became unbearable; it was clear she was in agony and, finally, the teacher stopped and turned his attention towards her and said, 'My dear, I must tell you, you are stealing everyone's experience, and your decision to do so is selfish. Why do you choose this path, and disrupt this moment?' The room was silent, shocked faces throughout. I do not think anyone had expected this to be his response.

She looked up through her swollen, red eyes and said, 'Can you not see I am in pain?' The teacher responded, 'No, I cannot see pain, I can only see your suffering.' She got up abruptly and ran out of the room and, without a further moment of concern, the teacher turned his attention back to the rest of the room and continued on.

Many years later, I still return to this moment, wondering if this could have been handled differently. I do not think this woman intended to create such a disruption. To me, her misery was a cry for help and a yearning for compassion. But looking at the lesson within this experience, was this woman really in pain, or was she, as the teacher said, in a suffering state? Could this woman suffer, but be without pain?

When pondering this, perhaps we can look to science. If this woman were to visit a doctor and say, 'Doctor, I am in pain, please help me,' he might respond, 'Please tell me where it hurts. What is the source of your injury?' This woman might say, 'It is my heart, it aches, I am in so much pain,' but, upon investigation, the doctor would not find any physical injury; it does not exist. Now this does not mean that the woman is not being truthful, and if she is hurting, then, to her, the feelings are real – but in actuality, this is not pain she is feeling but instead suffering. It is her heart that is broken, not her bones.

So, you may wonder, then, what is suffering, if it is not pain? And is it an inevitability or a choice? I have come to believe it is the latter. Suffering is the story we attach to our traumatic experiences, it is the legacy of emotions we burden ourselves with, dwelling in the misery of our past misfortunes, painful or otherwise. And as unpleasant and uncomfortable as it is to suffer, it is still a conscious choice we make: we choose to be a victim and we choose to prolong the story. In all cases of suffering, give it permission to exist.

So why, then, do we choose to suffer? I, too, have asked this of myself many times, and I am not foreign to the sufferings in my own past. I believe that we choose suffering because it allows us to disperse ownership of our traumas and sadness, to find something or someone to blame. When we suffer, we can say, 'My ex-boyfriend has ruined my life,' or 'This illness means I will never walk again,' and we can have an outlet for our angers and frustrations. This can be a very cathartic process, but it does not help us heal. It only helps us to hold on.

Here is a sequence for relieving suffering:

Acknowledgement – We cannot ignore our feelings; if we do, they linger and can steal our wellbeing. If your body has been injured or you are experiencing illness, you must not ignore it. If you are heartbroken or feeling taken advantage of, acknowledging your feelings is the first step to healing.

Acceptance – Suffering and grief are real experiences, so give it a name, acknowledge the situation, speak about it as truth. Acceptance is a step towards reality, a surrendering to what is, what has been done. It will likely be tough, but try not to assign blame. Speak about your suffering not as something that was done 'to you' but simply as something that was done.

Action – Do not allow yourself to dwell on the misery of your misfortunes. You have come this far in your healing, and forgiveness occurs with considered action. At first, when speaking of your hardship speak about these things in the past tense, as things behind you. Do not say you are heartbroken, but instead say you are 'on the path to healing'. From here, have a conversation with the person who has hurt you – it is probably long overdue – or if your injury is physical, make a plan for your rehabilitation and do not wait any longer to begin. Create a vision for the future that celebrates your progress. When we act purposefully, emotions will ease.

Suffering exists only if we allow the attachments of the past to become the stories of the present. Choose to be here now, and suffering cannot exist.

Wisdom is knowing what
is not needed, and leaving
behind what is not wanted

WE MUST LEARN TO MOURN, AND THEN MOVE ON

Children have a way of simplifying life. One time, when I was visiting a friend, I was looking after her young boy while she was out at the store collecting some things for dinner that night. His name was Harper and he was maybe five years old at the time. He was a rugged child, often rolling in the dirt, chasing after bees and bugs and whatever he could find buried in the grass. On that particular day, we were out in the garden when he managed to catch a cricket that was jumping around in the weeds, and he came to show me, the little creature nestled between the cups of his hands. He had a big smile on his face and was overjoyed. He asked if he could keep it and, not wanting to make that decision on my own, I said that we needed to ask his mother when she got back from town, and so, for the time being, he should just enjoy the company of his new friend.

A short while later, his mother returned home and, when she joined us in the garden, Harper ran to her in excitement. 'Look, Mummy, I have made a new friend!' His mother, with a warm smile, said back, 'I am so happy for you. Enjoy your time together playing in the garden.' And so, for the afternoon, we all sat in the garden as Harper played with his new cricket friend. He placed it in an empty box he had found nearby and, attempting to make it a more comfortable home, he added sticks and weeds he pulled from the garden. He even ran inside to fetch a piece of lettuce from the kitchen to feed it. He was beaming with joy; this was perhaps the greatest moment of his young life so far.

As the afternoon folded to a close, it was time to go inside; dinner time was fast approaching and everyone needed to get ready for supper. His mother said, 'Harper, it's time to pack up and come in for dinner.'

Inevitably, he asked, 'Can I bring my cricket inside? I'll keep him in my room so that we can play tomorrow.' He had grown quite attached to this new friend and so this question was not a surprise. 'No, my darling, you may not. He can't come into the house, you must leave him out in the garden with the other crickets. Otherwise, he'll miss his own supper.' Being only five years old, this answer was not well received, and immediately frustration followed, with Harper becoming distraught and heartbroken. Tears flowed, screaming and crying could be heard throughout the house, and eventually his mother picked him up and carried him in, leaving the cricket outside in the garden. The little boy was angry and inconsolable for some time thereafter.

Later that evening, after he had washed, ready for bed, it was clear that Harper's mood had changed completely: he was very happy, laughing, giggling and playing with the toys in his room. This intrigued me, so I asked him, 'Harper, do you still miss your cricket friend?' This may not have been the wisest choice, bringing this up so close to bedtime, but I asked anyway, even though I am sure his mother would not have approved.

His answer was concise but profound. 'I've finished crying. I was sad, but now I've moved on.'

There are times in our lives when we must ensure that we take time to mourn for what has been lost. This is important, and it is a necessary process when we are grieving a great loss or travesty. Whether it is a relationship that has ended, a lost dream or a lost soul, it is a necessary step to feel our feelings and let our emotions rise. This will help to bring closure in painful times. But the wisdom in this story is that we cannot mourn for ever and, at some point, it must end. For some people, the idea of 'moving on' is hard to accept because it can feel like we are giving up or devaluing our relationships or experiences. But we must also know we are not, and it is simply not fair to believe that moving on is a wrongdoing or an unjust action. If we do not eventually move on, it can paralyse us and impede future moments of joy and meaningful experiences. Do not deprive yourself of this possibility. You are never undeserving of happiness.

If this helps, my thoughts are this: take time to mourn, do it passionately and completely, allow yourself to feel all the emotions that arise, do not quell your heartache. Do not rush this process, and do not suppress any feelings as they come up; feel them all and take time to process them. Perhaps, like Harper, if need be, throw a tantrum; let the anger have its moment. For a moment is all that it will be if you truly let yourself indulge. Remember you are never too old for tears.

But then, as the frustration begins to subside, and it will, make the choice to move on. This does not need to be done in haste, and it does not mean you need to forget. If it is easier to do so, make this transition in a celebratory or ceremonial way, as a moment of recognition can help to end the mourning.

The first time you do this process, it will probably be difficult. Detachment is a cause for suffering for many people, but in time and with gentleness, it will become easier, and it is always for the better in the long term. A lost loved one, they would not want you to commiserate their life if it stops you from living yours.

In moments of mourning, be like Harper. Mourn and then move on, and you'll find the strength to let go and find your peace.

Today I will remember, but
tomorrow is a new day, so I will
not live like it is yesterday

WE ONLY SEE SHADOWS
WHEN FACING THE PAST

An endless shadow,
The familiar darkness stirs,
Behind you is spring.

Healing begins when
attachment ends

STEP FIVE
THE TRIANGLE FOLD

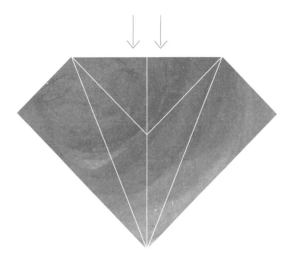

In this step we only have one small fold to make, the triangle fold, but do not think that it is not worth your full attention, as it is an essential fold to shape the body of your crane. Start by opening the top flaps of the kite on one side of the shape; this will return one side of your shape to a diamond. Take a moment to acknowledge the folded flaps on the back side of the kite; this will form a line across the back which will be a helpful guide when creating the front fold. When you are ready, carefully fold down the top corner of the kite towards the centre of the diamond, feeling the fold line on the back as an indicator for where the crease will land. Once it is aligned, take a moment to run your fingers along the crease, deepening and firming the fold, then unfold it.

For steps where it is necessary to subsequently unfold, I find it helpful, once it is unfolded, to run my fingers along the reverse crease to ensure that it returns to its unfolded state. The crease itself will stay intact, but the fold itself will soften. Now flip the crane over and repeat on the back side to ensure that the triangle is folded both ways. Once you have unfolded the top of the kite after the second side, return the outer corners (B & D) back to the centre on both sides, returning to the original kite shape and ready for what comes next.

PATIENCE

EMBRACING UNCERTAINTY

I do not think anyone is so saintly that they have not felt the scorn of impatience once before. It is a bite that comes in haste, often unplanned, rearing its head in a moment of frustration and ego. And so, we must ask ourselves, why is it that we lose our patience? Or maybe, why can we not keep it in times of anger or unrest? When we speak of patience, we often do not speak of the experience of having it, but in fact of what it feels like to lose it.

But this itself can be a wonderful realization, because how can we lose something if it is not already within us? Patience is the practice of embracing uncertainty and holding, above all else, our peace as a sacred endeavour. And so, patience is the practice to prolong the moments when we are calm and at ease and cultivate a trusting nature in the wisdom that naturally resides within. Time is our greatest commodity, and patience is our commitment to walk slowly in its footsteps.

A hurried mind will choose
the fewest steps, a patient
one will enjoy many

DO NOT FOLD
UNDER PRESSURE

When facing the pressures of life, we must learn to protect our peace. And this is the case not just for folding paper, but is also something to remember when faced with challenging and frustrating situations. It is not enough to simply hope for reprieve; instead, we must actively seek out a patient way of being. This, of course, may be easier said than done. As humans, we are attracted to our negativities and inadequacies, and we can find it hard to see any positivity amidst our challenges and disappointments, even if there is an abundance of good that surrounds the same occasion. But often, even the smallest acknowledgement of progress can be a powerful step towards an understanding perspective. And when done, can help to establish a kinder way of moving through the world.

I have found that these three practices are helpful reminders in times when we feel the uprising of impatience.

More effort may not help

Not every situation will benefit from more effort or force, but often, when we feel the pressure of a challenging situation, our first instinct is to put up a fight, work harder or push through it. On some occasions, this may even make the situation worse. In times of frustration, understand that you may not need to do more; instead, cultivate qualities that can offer support in this moment, compassion for your efforts, courage in your attempts, gratitude at doing your best; and recognition of how far you have come.

Act, don't react

Take a moment to pause and exhale: do not feel the need to resolve your challenges immediately. Often, when pressured, our first reaction is to resolve the situation and find relief from it quickly, for it is not in our nature to be comfortable in discomfort. But be warned: this can lead to emotional reactions rather than a considered response, and decisions made in moments of trepidation are governed by our fears and insulted egos. And so, we must take time to let our emotions settle. I often like to think of a hasty reaction as a regrettable action (re-action), something done without greater consideration, so it is important to give way and make space so that we can respond with purposeful actions. Before you react, just breathe.

Learn to walk away

There is a common misconception that giving up is a sign of weakness. But this is not true: knowing when to walk away or change direction is a powerful insight. Having time away from certain people, removing yourself from an unkind situation, or walking away completely because it is no longer for you, this is a sign of wisdom and growth. Give yourself the permission to prioritize your peace; when you do this, your world will soften.

In haste all edges sharpen,
in time they soften

TAKE TIME FOR TEA

In Japan, tea is more than just a hot drink, it is a sacred ritual of tranquillity and presence. Traditionally shared ceremonially, each element is crafted meticulously, from how it is prepared and poured to how it is sipped and enjoyed. Each stage in the process takes significant time, for it is the practice of complete presence and absolute attention. The act of tea should never be rushed.

And so, when preparing tea, no matter the occasion, consider every cup as your own little sacred ritual. Take time to slow down and enjoy the full experience, knowing that the whole experience is a beautiful and mindful practice.

FIVE PETALS
TEA MEDITATION

Here is a tea meditation that you may like to try at home. It is a practice of the five senses and one that I do myself most mornings when drinking tea.

The first petal, sight: *The moment of beginning*

When beginning the ritual of tea, start by setting the table, laying out purposefully the items and objects you will need to create your cup of tea: place your teacup and teapot on the table in front of you, gather any utensils you will need, perhaps a small spoon or napkin. And then select your tea leaves, or teabag and place these also delicately in front of you.

Once everything is laid out, step back and see what is unfolding. Be present in this moment and be appreciative of the time. See the delicacy and beauty of each item. Notice the texture and details. Do not rush into action; instead, be grateful for what each piece offers to the experience. Allow yourself to see everything; let this moment be enough on its own.

The second petal, sound: *Preparing the tea*

As you begin to prepare your tea, allow the sound of each item to take your focus in its own unique way. Notice the sound of the tea being scooped or the teabag dropped, listen to the water pouring, the spoon and the cup dancing in tandem, each offering its own moment for you to appreciate. Often, each sound alone is soothing and inviting, and together, these moments are a symphony of sounds, creating a gentle opus for your ears.

The third petal, touch: *Brewing the tea*

During the brewing process, allow yourself to focus on the physical touch of the tea. Perhaps place your hands around the cup to feel the warmth. Be gentle, so as not to disrupt the settling of the brew. You may also lean in over the tea and let the rising steam kiss your cheeks. Let the tea touch your skin; in doing so, it will touch your soul.

Now that your tea is brewing, there is nothing else to do: just let it be. There is no substitute for letting tea have its moment to awaken, and so we must be patient and give it the necessary time. Often this will take a few minutes, and if you are impatiently waiting, then this time will feel like an eternity. Instead, use this moment for gratitude, and be appreciative of this moment to pause.

The fourth petal, smell: *Experiencing the tea*

Once the tea has had time to develop, allow yourself to experience the tea through its aromas. Let every cup be special, uniquely blended to soften the sensations, know that this moment will never be repeated; make space to be here completely. Do not rush to sip; instead, breathe it in. Smell is linked to the quality of our breath, so inhale each aroma completely and exhale into a space of calm and quietude. This is the power of scent and sensation.

The fifth petal, taste: *Enjoying the tea*

In arriving at the fifth petal of your tea meditation, do not consider this the pinnacle, so do not make more of this moment than the others: it is simply the last sensation to be enjoyed and one to be experienced equally to all the previous stages. As you take your first sip, notice how it feels and how you feel. Notice what you taste; sip it slowly; let the flavours unfold. In doing so, we can appreciate the time and process of fully committing to this moment.

Never rush a cup of tea,
for it only knows one way

WISDOM IS THE GIFT,
TIME IS THE RIBBON

When facing a challenging experience, our greatest opportunity is the gift of time. Sometimes we can be misled to think that if we work harder, keep going or act stronger, we may overcome the obstacles that block our path, but true progress is knowing when to step back and give ourselves the chance to breathe.

Patience itself can be experienced in a few different ways, and we must recognize that we can have very different experiences of time itself. I will often speak of patience in four stages: regret, anticipation, acceptance and enlivenment. Each is a completely different experience. This is the wisdom of cultivating a consistent practice of patience.

Let us use the metaphor of catching a train. Imagine that you are running late for work and you have hastily made your way to the station, only to just miss the train as it pulls away. And your only option is to wait for the next one to arrive. You look at the schedule and realize that it will be another fifteen minutes before the next one, which means you now must wait. The question is, how will you spend this time?

Regretting is re-living the negativity of the past and seeing this time as a punishment for our past actions. When waiting for the train, you will be frustrated by all the choices you made up until this moment. Why did you get up so late? Why did you take so long getting ready? Why did you stop to take that photo on the way to the station? Regardless of the decisions you made up until that point, every one of them is regrettable and caused delay. This type of waiting will probably make the experience miserable and upsetting. If you find yourself in this state of regret, simply acknowledge that time is unchangeable, return to the state of what is, instead of what you should have done, and do not waste your energy becoming distraught.

Anticipating is an untrusting tolerance of the time ahead, thinking only of the future and catastrophic events. When we are in a state of anticipating, we will also experience doubt and fear; our mind will attach to the uncertainty of the unknown.

When waiting for the train, you will be doubtful of the sequence of events that will come next. Will the next train be on time? Will there be space for me on it? Will it go fast enough so that I can still make it to my destination on time? When waiting with anticipation, we find ourselves always in a state of anxiousness and anticipation, feeling as if the future cannot come fast enough.

Accepting is a reasonable endurance of what is, without the attachment of needing the situation to be good or bad. When we are accepting of the time, we are not shackled by the past or the future, we are simply present and in the moment, accepting that time must pass, and that it is what it is.

When waiting for the train, being in a state of acceptance is being present to the circumstance but unattached to the expectations that may rise or fall because of it. We do not feel the need to ask questions, for we already know the answer. We have simply accepted that time must run its course, and then, when the train arrives, we will get on and head to work.

Living is a shift in perspective towards positive action and the appreciation that this time is a gift and can be well spent. When we are living patiently we recognize all moments as blessings and we only see opportunities, not obstacles.

When waiting for the train, we may use this time to appreciate the fresh air, start a pleasant conversation with a stranger, use the moment to call a loved one or take a quiet moment of meditation. These choices are positive actions: choose to see these waiting moments as a gift worthy of gratifying actions.

And so, we must always remember that to be patient is the practice of embracing uncertainty with kindness and perspective. This is the gift and wisdom of time well spent.

A moment of gratitude is
always time well spent

THE SEASHELL FOLD

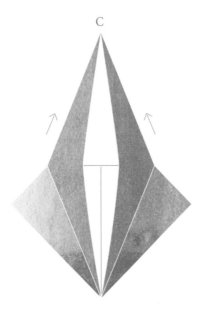

In this step, start by unfolding the flaps of the kite and open the paper back into the diamond-square shape. Do this one side at a time, first the front in its entirety, then flip it over to complete the back side. To begin, start by lifting the bottom corner of the top folded layer (C), revealing the belly of the fold. At the centre of the belly will be the strong crease that you made earlier, in step 5, while constructing the top of the kite. Press a finger along this inside crease to firm the centre of the fold. You should start to see the shape of the seashell forming in front of you. Take your time not to rush this step; it can be tricky, and you may need the support of all your fingers to delicately manoeuvre this fold into place.

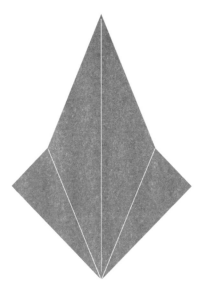

The next part has always been the most difficult for me personally: folding the outer corners of the seashell towards the midline of the shape. I prefer to do this one side at a time, very slowly and intentionally, taking the time not to rush the step. What can make this fold difficult is that we are inverting folds, which means we are creating reverse folds with creases that were first folded in the opposite direction. Move each outer corner towards the centre of the seashell, thus creating a new outer edge. Press firmly along the outline of the new seashell shape. If the previous folds were not precise, then it is here that we will see their inaccuracies. Do not let this unravel how far you have come. At this point, you are halfway through, but do not rush to do the second side. Take time to appreciate this abstract form, an unconventional shape in the traditional symmetry of paper folding. It is a vast transformation and a necessary reminder that we do not all need to be of a certain fit or form. You'll finish the fold in the next chapter.

RESILIENCE

REMEMBERING WHY

It is an inevitability of life to get knocked down, and when this happens we can believe that this is our end, and that we have been defeated. But this is not true, for we can only be beaten if we do not rise, and this is a choice only you alone can make. Resilience is the practice of remembering why we started in the first place and keeping this in our hearts through challenges and obstacles that cross our path.

Be kind to yourself; do not distract yourself with miseries or misfortunes: healing takes time and needs to be unrushed. Unburden yourself of expectations and simply allow yourself the space to find your strength; wander back to your path and keep moving forward. Nothing can defeat you without your permission: remember why and continue to rise.

RISE LIKE THE TIDE

Waves flow in rhythm,
Darkness brings the falling rain,
Remember the sun.

The beauty is remembering not
when the sun will rise, but why

REST OFTEN,
BUT DO NOT GIVE UP

Five Restful Practices for Resilience

We must all cultivate a resilient nature that will keep us strong and supported. A well-rested spirit will result in purposeful actions and wise choices.

And so, in times of hardship, we must not give up, but we must learn to rest, because this is the most powerful path to restoration and replenishment. Never think of it as detrimental to our progress for it is the necessary resolve to rise back up. Rest is rest, a conscious action to unwind our stresses and empower our resilient actions.

Rest the body – Give yourself time to physically be still. If you are tired or worn down, sleep or take time to rest, minimize your actions and truly give yourself permission to do less.

Nothing will replace a good night's sleep, so go to bed earlier, or sleep longer in the morning, and do not judge the time you sleep; instead, appreciate the results of a restful night. Waking up early is not a sign of success; sleeping in late is not laziness. Rest is rest, and a well-rested body always rises with intention.

Rest the breath – Slow down and give your breath a calming focus. Try to create an even and easy rhythm. Conscious and coherent breathing will ease the nervous system and increases the quality of our inhalations and exhalations, enabling us to feel more capable and at peace. The *Even Breath* practice below will help.

Imagine your breath in four even parts:

1. The inhale
2. A pause and retention at the top with a full breath
3. The exhale
4. A pause and retention at the bottom with an empty breath

Now imagine your breath as a square box, each part slowly drawing up and along the sides of the square evenly so that the rhythm of your practice is steady and elongated.

Start your practice using a four-second count along each side of the square.

1. Inhale for four
2. Pause and hold the breath for four
3. Exhale for four
4. Pause and hold the breath for four

Repeat this practice for ten rounds, or set a timer for two to three minutes and practise continuously until the time ends. If you would like to practise longer, you can; this technique can be done for as long as you would like as it is beneficial to your peace. You may also like to increase the count of your inhales and exhales to six or even eight seconds. After you have finished, sit gently and notice the effects. How do you feel? By practising this technique, you will immediately find a calming sensation and a restful feeling. This is a great daily practice and one you can do any time in moments of stress or unrest.

Rest in the mind – Even at times when we are resting the body, it is easy to let the mind keep churning. On some occasions, when the body rests, the mind may even pick up speed and become overwhelmed with thought and turbulence. Unfortunately, it is not possible to switch off the mind. Do not let anyone convince you that it is: you are not a light switch; you do not have an 'on' and 'off' button. And so, we must actively cultivate a process in which we can quiet our mind and let ease be experienced intentionally.

One such technique to help you do this is meditation, a practice to minimize the distraction in our mind and experience a state of non-thinking. There are many styles of meditation, but one practice that may serve you well is the practice of Zazen, the 'sitting' practice. Zazen is popular in Japan and originates from Buddhist teachings, and the practice is regarded as a dedicated moment of complete presence and awareness.

To practise Zazen, find yourself a comfortable seat on the floor. It is customary to sit cross-legged, but if you find that this is uncomfortable or not possible, then adjust yourself to find a position that is comfortable for a dedicated amount of time. If this means sitting on a chair or a sofa, then that is OK. Select the seat that works for you and eases the body from physical discomfort. You may also find it comfortable to sit on a cushion or a pillow. If you are a person who gets cold easily, wrap yourself in a blanket so you do not get chilly during the time.

As you find your seat, allow your eyes to narrow and land gently on the floor just in front of you or, if you prefer, close your eyes. In traditional Zazen practice, you may be invited to sit a few centimetres away from the wall and allow your eyes to soften as you stare straight ahead.

The practice of Zazen is a practice of absolute awareness in the moment, a disengagement from the thoughts that will try to steal your attention. This is a practice of non-thinking and relentless attention, and when practised in a meaningful way, it will allow the mind to rest from the temptations of indulgent and distracting thoughts.

A Zazen practice is traditionally forty minutes, so if you can afford the time and have the willingness to practise, then it will serve you well to commit your attention for this period of time. However, this can be quite long when first starting, so I would suggest beginning with less time or a length of time that suits you well. Always remember that any time is better than no time, so do not feel you must practise for a certain length of time to receive the benefits.

If you are new to meditation practice, then I would suggest starting with less time. Eight minutes is a meaningful amount of time when you are beginning. Practise this twice a day then slowly increase the time from eight minutes to twenty, and then, perhaps, you will find it valuable to sit for forty minutes. In time, you will find longer periods become more enjoyable to sit and be still.

Rest your emotions – Humans are emotional creatures and we can experience a full range of our feelings, from excitement to frustration, passion to distress, and countless other feelings that will impact our energy and capacity. If you are an empathetic person, the wave of emotions you feel can be exhausting and depleting.

And so, we must learn to calm the swinging emotions of life and move inwards towards equanimity and a state of emotional detachment. We must understand that, to rest our emotions, we must intentionally step away from dramatic moments and sensational experiences. When we choose to rest, we allow ourselves the time to reflect and feel a prolonged sense of ease. Often, we will find that the highs need not be so high and the lows are not as desolate as they may otherwise seem. When we give ourselves permission to rest, we gain a new perspective on our emotions that helps us differentiate between the needs of our attention and what is simply an emotional distraction.

Rest your spirit – In times of healing, we must hold on to a hopeful spirit, but this does not mean we cannot have moments of rest here too. Often, when we hold too tightly to hope or a healing path, it can become overwhelming if we do not loosen our grip and find reprieve, especially if our healing path is long. Often, being hopeful can feel all-consuming, especially if we are fighting an illness or recovering from injury, or if we are rising against injustice, and so, when we dedicate ourselves fully to our compassionate efforts, it can be exhausting. But even hopeful efforts must be given quiet moments; we must learn to trust that a moment to pause will not dilute or dissolve our resolve. In fact, when we allow ourselves a moment to rest, we can often find a renewed sense of purpose. Take time to rest, so our waking efforts may not be short-lived.

When climbing a mountain,
stop often for the view

I would rather a mouse
that roars than a lion
that says he will

THE WHISPER AND
THE ROAR

There once was a mouse who was tiny and small,
Who woke up each day to answer the call,
To take on the world with her strength and might,
To rise each day and continue her fight.

One day she met a lion who was fierce and strong,
Who doubted her courage to keep singing her song,
He said, 'You cannot roar, you are not like me,
'You are a mouse, you are small, and that's all you can be.'

But the mouse did not listen, she knew she could roar,
So, she opened her mouth and stretched her jaw to the floor,
She let out a sound, but nothing did stir,
For the roar she let out was just a quiet whisper.

The lion laughed in her face and told her to give up,
He said, 'Your voice would not fill even the smallest teacup,
'Tomorrow I will show you a real lion's roar,'
But the next morning all he did was continue to snore.

But the mouse did not quit, she continued to try,
She never gave up and she never did cry,
But at night when she slept and laid her head down,
She vowed that every day she would continue her sound.

And even though she had a small little voice,
It is the willingness to try which is the bravest choice,
Because it is not the volume that defines your roar,
But the courage inside that encourages more.

Do not doubt the journey,
a circle always returns home

STEP SEVEN
THE DIAMOND FOLD

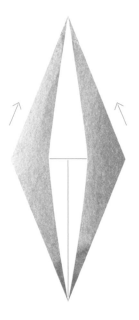

Do not rush this stage – perhaps, even, this is a good moment to pause and take rest. I have found many times that the seashell fold has frustrated me; it is complex, so the challenges can endure. A moment to pause is never unwelcome. The second seashell fold is often more familiar, and you will inevitably get better. Now, you may wonder, why does this fold require a whole step of its own? This, for some, could easily be a simple instruction to fold the second side of the seashell like the first. But I have found that, for many people, this is the step that requires further consideration, and a moment to pause between sides can calm any frustration in the fingertips created on the first side.

C

When you are ready, flip your crane over and prepare to fold the second side of the seashell to make the diamond fold. Begin by lifting the bottom point (C) up to reveal the belly of the crane once again. As you lift the bottom point, trace the crease of the inside fold to ground the opening, and then press the outer corners together, one at a time, and trace the long edges of the seashell to sharpen and finish the fold. Once you have done both flaps, you should find yourself with a hidden gem in your hand, a beautiful diamond almost ready to fly.

SUPPORT

LOVE IN ACTION

I am often asked for guidance in times when someone has lost their way or has reached a point where they feel helpless and undone. And on these occasions, I will do my best to share kind words and offer support where I can, knowing that everyone often simply needs love and kindness. For the most part, I will ask them to be gentler and let them speak about their troubles, as I have learned that most people just want to be heard and know that someone else cares for their wellbeing.

To give support is a sign of love, and to receive it is a sign of connection. Sometimes, asking for help can feel like we are giving up, but this is not true: asking for help is deciding that we are not yet willing to do so. Do not allow this to be misunderstood. And do not push away support; allow others to help you as you would likely help them.

Life is not a path to be walked alone, and we must cultivate strong relationships that make us feel safe and give us a sense of belonging. To be in such a relationship with someone else, or a community of people, is to understand that, together, we can do far more than we can alone. Support is the practice of love in action, to give it, receive it and be it, for ourselves and for others.

Like cranes that fly together in a flock, so, too, should humans when travelling through life.

A strong yoke carries
a heavier load

AN OUTSTRETCHED HAND

When we were young boys, my brother and I would often get into fights when we could not resolve our disagreements with words alone. As we were only two years apart, there were many times our differences resulted in frustration and anger and, like boys do, punches were thrown and tears followed. But no matter the argument or who came out victorious, my father would always stand us up and make us shake hands, apologize to each other and say, 'I love you.' Regardless of who won or lost the fight, an outstretched hand was always the way any disagreement was resolved.

It has been many years since our last bout and, like most children, we have grown out of our childhood immaturity, but from time to time, as you might expect, my brother and I still fall into spirited debate and disagreement. Often it is trivial, such as differing perspectives about the proper technique to use when steaming a fish or folding dumplings. But still to this day, after any disagreement, we will shake hands, to ensure no real love has been lost.

I think a great misfortune in life is believing that a fist is stronger than an outstretched hand. A hand, when closed, is unwilling to bond or find common ground for connection. When we make a fist, decency and resolution are lost. A fist is such a primitive tool, one rooted in aggression and division: we close our fists to fight battles and wars, to segregate our opinions and to display the acts of a flagrant ego.

It may seem that a fist is strong, but it is not real strength, it is simply the most common. While a fist may be able to resolve the past, it cannot welcome the present or unite our future. When we make a fist, it is an action of finality and resistance, one that accepts disagreement and divide. Even in the ring when two fighters are in battle, it is common to see them outstretch a hand at the conclusion, no matter the outcome.

But a fist cannot show love, for it holds our pride too tightly in our clenched hands, unwilling to let go or find a place of agreement. A closed hand cannot help someone when they have been knocked to the floor, nor can it offer a seat to a stranger with tired feet. Only an open hand can greet a friend or wave a fond farewell.

An open hand is a sign of connection and invitation; it is literally a helping hand outstretched with love. An open hand asks nothing in return, but unites two people in a bonded progress. And when carrying a heavy load, it is helpful to have support; many hands make light work, and an open hand is always an offer of love.

An open hand is
always the strongest

THE INVISIBLE ARMY

One autumn night a few years back, our home was broken into while we were sleeping and many of our belongings were stolen. The thieves took our wallets, passports, cameras and other personal items that were lying around the house. The following day, my partner and I awoke to the aftermath and the police were called and reports filed. The next few days were filled with an overwhelm of emotions, our fears flooding our minds with a feeling of helplessness and hurt. Would the culprits be back? Were we still in danger? Could we afford to replace everything that had been stolen? Would we be able to sleep soundly again?

Over the next few days, as we spoke to neighbours and friends, the support we received was truly beautiful. Friends and loved ones from all over the world sent messages and kind words;

people I hadn't spoken to in years called asking if we were OK or needed help replacing the things we had lost. Our elderly neighbour, who is nearing ninety years old, offered to stand guard outside the house during the night so that we could sleep soundly, and family friends offered to lend us their teenage boys to sleep on the sofa for a few days in case anyone came back to try again. Over the next week, more and more messages poured in; people sent flowers and cards, cakes and small gifts; friends checked in just to see that we were OK and called back every night to make sure everything was safe and secure before we went to bed. It was a beautiful display of love and support, and something we had not expected on this scale. We had never felt so loved.

I have been reminded that, fundamentally, we are creatures of community and it is in our nature to ensure that others are OK. Even distance or time apart cannot dull the flames of friendship and the power of love, and people will continue to cheer us on even if we have lost touch or not seen them for a while. I have learned through this experience five things about support that remind me how much stronger we are together and how much impact a supportive environment can have on our wellbeing.

First, people are innately helpful and will always support where they can. In the case of hardship or misfortune, people will go to extraordinary lengths to ensure you feel safe and loved.

Second, we must remember to be proactive with our support. In our case, we did not overtly ask for help, but it came flooding in. Do not always wait for people to ask for your help; sometimes, their situation is too traumatic for them to reach out straight away. If you are able to, reach out often, call or send a message, and do not tire from trying; sometimes, it may take a few tries before someone is ready or able to accept your support, and that is OK. Be persistent and do not let your ego or emotions get in the way of your efforts; sometimes, their resistance itself is a cry for help. Support is often easier to give than it is to receive.

Third, never underestimate the power of real human connection. Pick up the phone to say hi and check in; in a digital world, there is nothing more warming than the sound of friends or family. Real support comes from real connections: do not be efficient when it comes to love and kindness.

The fourth thing is that when support is offered to you, try to say yes: do not let your pride get in the way. Almost everything in life is easier when the work is shared. If you are struggling to pay the rent, or make ends meet, be honest, share your troubles, and you will be pleasantly surprised at the lengths people will go to to help get you back on your feet. If you are struggling mentally or emotionally, do not feel you are a burden to others; you never need to suffer alone, there are always people who are happy to listen. Now, some people would say, do not accept support if you are unwilling to give, but I do not think this should be the case. Instead, simply accept with gratitude, be truly appreciative of someone's time, offering and energy.

And finally, support is not a measure of equal exchange, it is not an agreement of reciprocity or future repayment. Give it freely if you can, but do not expect anything in return. Support need not be rewarded; let it always simply be love in action.

Ultimately, we must remember that to be kind to others need not be a grand action or effort; a warm smile, a few kind words or simply the time to sit with a friend can be more than enough in someone's hour of need.

I am forever grateful knowing that I am loved, and I want you to know that you are loved, too.

The most beautiful
flowers are the ones
that grow together

LOVE IS ESSENTIAL,
BELONGING IS
UNCONDITIONAL

When I first moved to London in my late twenties, I did not have many close friends, so during my first Christmas I did not have anything particularly meaningful to do over the holidays. Being so far away from my family, who were all living in California at the time, it was agreed that it was too expensive to travel during this time of the year and that instead I would visit during quieter times, when flights were more affordable. And so, I found myself with no plans and no invitations at Christmas, something I had not experienced before in my life.

So, at the start of December, I began to look around for festive activities to do over the holiday period. I found many things on offer. I found a group of events called 'Orphan's Christmas', where local groups of friends hosted people living away from their families. This was nice; I had never heard of it before, but it was good to know such things existed, because the holiday season can be a lonely time for people who are away from their families. There were also many Christmas markets and late-night-shopping events, with concerts, shows, good music and delicious food. These also sounded interesting, but I knew that none of these felt right for me.

A few days later, I was walking down the road and saw a flyer in a shop window asking for volunteers to help at the local homeless shelter. This felt like a meaningful way to be of service, so I signed up. I selected three shifts at the shelter closest to my house and over the next few weeks attended the introductions and orientation training so that I knew what I would be doing.

My first shift was on Christmas Eve. I remember thinking how strange it felt not to be with my family but, at the same time, I was happy to be able to help in whatever way I could. Throughout that evening, I met many amazing people, volunteers and homeless guests alike. Everyone was just so grateful to be there, together, enjoying each other's company, sharing a meal, a laugh and endless stories. If you looked around the room, you wouldn't be able to tell who was a guest and who was a volunteer, it was simply a space full of people enjoying being together. No judgements, just joy. No one cared what you did for work, in part because most guests there did not have jobs. And no one cared how much money you had or where you lived, because these were topics that most of the guests were unable to relate to. It was a humbling experience to remove material things from the conversation and simply experience real human connection, unjudged and unlabelled.

Many of the men and women I met were there because of personal hardship or unfortunate situations: some were hiding from an abusive relationship or had fled a war-torn country;

some were troubled by drugs and alcohol; and some were just lost and had nowhere else to go. Even with all the hardships it was such a beautiful environment to be in. There was immense joy all around. Throughout the experience, I felt a sense of belonging such as I had never felt before: unjudged, appreciated and unconditionally loved. And I did my best to give as much as I was receiving.

Like most people, when signing up to volunteer or give time to a charity, if we are honest with ourselves, we are first signing up so that we can feel a sense of fulfilment: we like to feel that by doing something meaningful and giving our time to support others, then we will feel good, as service and support is a gift that rewards everyone.

There is no hierarchy to the human spirit: we are all of equal measure when we remove the labels and titles. When we come together, open and available to give and receive support, then the result is simple, unconditional love. It is an important step to belonging, knowing that you are loved for who you are, not for what you do.

It has been almost ten years since I moved to London, and I have been volunteering every year since. These days, I cannot imagine Christmas any other way: my time at the shelter always nourishes me and puts the year behind in perspective. This has been a great source of inspiration for my own wellbeing and teachings throughout the year.

Love is not an experience of passion,
but a commitment of support

THE FEATHER OF HOPE

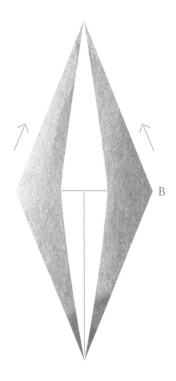

B

In front of you now is a long and elegant diamond shape. Start by taking the top layer of the right-side corner of the paper (B), fold the long edge of the paper diagonally upwards towards the middle of the shape so that the edges align in the middle: measure twice, fold once. Be firm in your fold and commit.

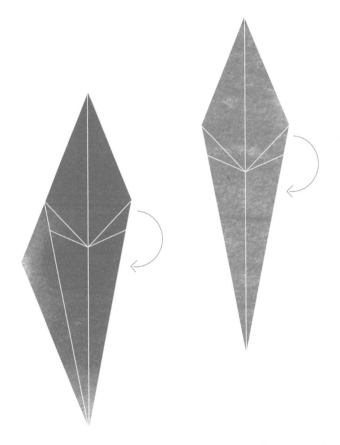

Once you are happy with this first flap, repeat the second flap folding the bottom left side inwards to the centre line. This should complete the top side of the shape. Pause, breathe, and when you're ready, continue. Flip your crane over and continue to the back-side folds. Repeat the steps from the front side, taking your time and letting the familiar folds from the first side guide the second set of inward folds.

You have arrived at the Feather of Hope.

Happiness Just Is. It is not a thing to find
or a destination to arrive at, it is, in fact,
simply the awareness to live in the moment
completely and the freedom to choose
wisely with your time.

Happiness is not something to hold in your
hand, it has no texture to touch, for it resides
in the heart and is felt within the soul.

In the final part of this book we explore the
qualities of happiness; gratitude, growth,
simplicity and joy. Each a meaningful step
towards a beautiful way of living.

FOLDS OF HAPPINESS

HAPPINESS

CELEBRATING THIS MOMENT

GRATITUDE
LOVE WITHOUT OPINION

In life, we are given the gift of perspective, and with this vision we must choose to see the world with appreciation and kindness. Be unconditional with your love and cultivate meaningful connections, give your time to the things that matter and learn from the things that have created resistance in the past, for there is nothing in this world that is undeserving of your gratitude. This is the gift of a kind mind and a loving heart.

Celebrate life as each
moment unfolds, there you
will find happiness

CRANE RETURNS
THE FAVOUR

There was once a man who lived alone and spent his days tending to his farm. One day when he was out in the fields, a beautiful white crane fell out of the sky and crashed into the field he was working in. Taking pity on the crane, the man went to the creature and noticed that an arrow had pierced its wing, so the man removed the arrow and cleaned the wound of the injured crane. In time, the bird was able to fly again and, as it flew away, it circled in the sky three times, as if to say thank you for the kindness.

On that same night, a beautiful woman appeared at the man's home, saying that she would be his wife and together they would live a happy life. Now, the man was very poor and did not have much money, so he told the woman that he could not support or feed her well and that she may want to reconsider being his wife. But she was still willing and said she had a bag of rice that would feed them and fill their stomachs. And so, as they began their life together, every day the man would cook them rice, but the bag would feed them both and fill their stomachs. The man was astonished, but very grateful.

One day, the woman told the man that she was going into another room to make something for him, but that he should not enter the room and should wait for her to return. Days passed and she did not come out. Eventually, a week later, she emerged with a beautiful and colourful piece of clothing she had made. She was tired, frail and looked very thin. She gave the piece of clothing to the man and told him to go into town the next day and sell it for a very good price. The next day, he returned home with more money than he had ever had in his whole life. He was now a wealthy man.

That night, she went back into the room once again, and again she told the man not to enter, but this time the man could not contain his curiosity. He wanted to know how she could weave such beautiful garments without any thread, and so he turned the key and peeked in. But when he looked into the room, his wife was nowhere to be found and, instead, there was the crane, plucking its own feathers to weave the cloth.

The crane turned around and realized that her true identity had been discovered. She told the man, 'I am the crane that you saved in the field. I became your wife to repay you for your love and kindness. But now that you know who I truly am, I cannot stay.' And she flew away, never to return.

This is the Japanese folklore tale *Tsuru no Ongaeshi* ('Crane Returns the Favour'), a story about gratitude, sacrifice and support. What I find most beautiful about this story is the offering of love and selflessness that the crane showed the man in return. She supported the man who saved her life and sacrificed her wellbeing so that he could be happy. The crane did not want credit for her actions, she only wanted to support this man and return the love that was shown to her.

As for the man, he teaches us that we should be grateful for what is offered, for if his curiosity or mistrust had been better managed, he would not have lost the love of his wife. Often, when we are shown acts of kindness, the ultimate act of gratitude is acceptance: not needing anything more. Especially with people close to you, trust that their love is sincere and simply be grateful for the love that is shared.

Love is a gift that
needs no reward

PERSPECTIVE IS THE
GREATEST BEAUTY

When I was a young boy, I experienced an asthma attack when visiting a neighbour's house; they had just got a new cat. As a boy, I was allergic to many things growing up – dogs, cat dander, dust mites, feather pillows, certain types of grass, and much more – and being around any of these things, even for just a moment, would trigger my allergies and, inevitably, an asthma attack would follow. On this occasion, I had not expected there to be a cat in the house – my mother always made sure to ask before I went anywhere new – but since I had been there many times before, this occasion could not have been planned for.

When I first arrived at the neighbours', I did not know the cat was there – perhaps it was in another room, or taking a nap in the sun – but immediately I could feel its presence, and it triggered my allergies, and my asthma escalated quickly. I remember feeling it coming on. Often, there is a small window of time between when it starts and when it becomes quite serious. And any joy in my body quickly turned to fear, laughs quickly turned to wheezing, the wheezing into gasping for air. I tried using my asthma inhaler a few times – the blue one, I never left home without it – but it did not help. An attack was imminent. Allergies are bad enough, but when combined with asthma, they can be quite dangerous. If you have ever experienced one yourself, or been around someone who has, you know that it is a frightening situation, the feeling of life being sucked out of your body while you struggle to find just enough air to survive. I would not wish this experience on anyone.

My mother was quickly called and I was carried home in tears, unable to breathe, traumatized and struggling for each gasp of air. I had had these attacks before and I lived in fear of these moments.

The remedy for an asthma attack back in the mid-eighties was to be hooked up to a nebulizer breathing machine, a motorized device about the size of a shoe box with an oxygen hose attached to it that led to what I can only describe as a plastic kazoo at the other end which held the medication. You would hold this in your mouth and breathe through it with long, slow, deep breaths and, in time, the breath would return. All the while, my mother would sit with me, gently stroking my back. 'Just breathe,' she would say. 'Just breathe.' The process to come down from the attack took twenty to thirty minutes, a lifetime when every breath feels like your last.

My doctor would always tell me to slow down, be gentle and not get overexcited. Sports and exhaustion were other triggers for my asthma, and so my life growing up was always modified to a gentler pace. All my friends were allowed to run around and have fun, and I was often not allowed to participate; it felt like a punishment. There were many times when I missed out on activities or experiences because of my asthma, and visiting friends' houses or going out on adventures always had to be 'asthma appropriate'. I always felt as if my childhood was diluted by my disease.

But like most things, as I have got older, I have also become wiser, and I can choose to see my childhood with a positive perspective. Because of my asthma, I was gifted a big head start on a quieter life. From an earlier age, I learned how to live life with less stimulation and less agitation, and how to remove myself from situations that were not serving my mental health and physical wellbeing. Because of my asthma, I know the value of a calm and easeful breath, knowing first hand the travesty of being without it. These days, when the world around me feels restless and relentless, or I begin to feel triggered or agitated, I will always quickly remove myself from these situations and step away to a quieter corner so I can return to my peace. Above all else, I have realized that the essence of my gentleness was the gift of growing up this way. Time and perspective have a way of changing how we see things, and for that I am grateful.

Misery will remind you what
you have lost, gratitude will
show you what you have learned

A GIFT TAKES
MANY SHAPES

I keep at my home a sketchbook of blank paper so that I can reach for it any time my mind wanders into fantasy or my eyes find beauty that I wish to hold on to for longer. And in these moments, I will grab my pencil and begin to draw, sitting quietly and letting my hands follow the lines of my inspiration. I have always wanted to be a great artist, but my hands have had other plans and, often, what I see and what I draw do not match; in fact, it is quite disproportionate at times, and I laugh to myself at how poor my artistry can be. But I do not sketch to create something beautiful but rather to feel the beauty that it creates within me.

When I first started drawing, I would make quick work of my sketches so as not to lose the spark of inspiration. I would be urgent with my attention and quick with my hands, but doing it this way, I never found joy. What I had created never matched what I saw in the way I had hoped and, over time, my expectations suffocated my experiences and I would easily give up because there was no pleasure to be found. In time, I learned that art is not the practice of outcomes, and nor should life be. But the journey to this perspective took some time. We must be grateful for the joy that it brings and the calm that it creates, but often this happens only when we slow down and detach from the results. Art, by definition, is subjective, and each person's creativity will vary, but if done with time and a quiet ego, then the experience should always be a gratifying endeavour.

Like many things in life, it is easy to find fault in what we lack and shift our focus to our deficits instead of our discoveries. In truth, my hands may always lack the delicacy to draw fine lines and deep shadows, but this will not change the peace I find in sitting down with my sketchbook and taking the time to be grateful for whatever comes out.

If you cannot find something
to be thankful for, you are
moving too fast

STEP NINE
THE CHOPSTICK FOLD

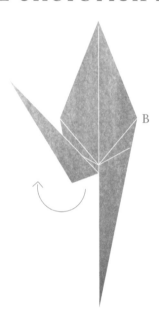

B

Like a caterpillar emerging from its cocoon, it is here that we may start to feel a sense of true transformation. This is the step where we can begin to see our crane come to life. It is often only when the first buds of spring blossom that we appreciate the efforts of the winter. Begin the chopstick fold by holding the base of the crane with your left hand, and then press your thumb and first finger together at the corner of the diamond (B) and gently let them run down the long edge over the folded terrain beneath. If you go slowly, you will be able to feel underneath where the paper will go from three layered folds to two; this is about a third of the way down the long edge. When you feel this spot, stop and press firmly.

To make the fold, flip your fingers so your thumb is on the underside of the paper and your index finger is now on top. Create a gentle crease as you begin to fold the first chopstick upwards at a diagonal. This fold has the most room for artistry and creativity, and you have the freedom to decide the angle of the fold. Once you have done the first side, flip your crane over and repeat the step for the second chopstick. This is often the fold that is said to create the personality of the crane. The wider the angle of the fold, the deeper your crane will bow; the narrower the angle, the more inspired it will stand.

GROWTH

THE INSIGHTS OF CHANGE

The world is forever changing; very little remains constant, and so we must continually learn to adapt to the waves of transformation. If change is abrasive and disregards the direction of our journey, this can be difficult to accept, especially if we are challenged by the scale or immediacy that it demands. Though we cannot control the rhythms of change, we can always choose how we respond. The beauty of a changing world is that it is inevitable, but as each moment unfolds, we must choose to expand and grow.

NOTHING GOOD HAPPENS
AFTER MIDNIGHT

As children, we are given many rules by our parents, but often we are too young to understand their purpose at the time. Growing up, my father was a firm but fair man, and within the walls of the family home there were certain rules that were expected to be followed. By the time I became a teenager, as you would expect, I was not fond of many of them, because rules limited my sense of freedom, both literally and figuratively, and to the ego of an adolescent mind, they simply did not make sense.

Looking back, there was one such rule that was always the cause of great turbulence between my father and me, and it was the rule for evening curfew. In his mind, it was simple: no matter the day or the reason, you must be home by midnight. There were no exceptions to this rule. It didn't matter if you were out studying for a test or out with friends, failure to make it home would result in a lecture and the punishment of additional chores.

Now, my father was not a preacher, but he could give a lecture like it was his divine right, and any time I or either of my siblings arrived home after the clock struck midnight, we knew we'd be in for it. He would always say, 'Nothing good happens after midnight,' a message that has stayed with me throughout my life and one that I have heard him say more times than I can count or remember. Luckily, my older brother, Andrew, was worse than I was when it came to arriving home on time so, often, my crimes were less harsh compared to those of the greater culprit who arrived home after me. However, on these occasions, if neither of us was home by midnight, I, being the first back, would have to sit in the living room awaiting his arrival so that my father would not need to waste his breath twice in the same evening.

Now that I am older, I look back fondly on these early years and the lessons I learned along the way. My father, who is now a gentler man, and I, a far less irreverent spirit, often laugh about those times when I would miss curfew and be reprimanded with 'the speech'. A few years back, I asked him why this was the one rule that he was so strict on. He laughed and, before he responded, he asked me what I thought now that I was older.

At first, my response was automatic. I had heard his lecture many times before, so I knew that being out late at night at that age usually meant nothing but trouble. He responded by agreeably reminding me that, as a teenager, there is very little to do past midnight; you are of course too young to go to a bar or a nightclub, you have already eaten dinner, cinemas and other common hangouts like the bowling alley or the arcades close around midnight, and so, inevitably, there was nowhere

You cannot chase your dreams
unless you are well rested

purposeful for us to be. If you were to ask me when I was seventeen years old, I would have argued otherwise, but such is the gift of time that certain opinions I would have had back then have since faded.

He said, 'It may not have seemed like much to you back then, but every minute you were late was a minute less sleep you would get. And when you come home late, you are not prolonging your day, but sacrificing your rest.'

Often, when we are younger and filled with exuberance, sleep is seen as negotiable rather than essential. Perhaps even now as you have got older this still may be the case. If we are having a good time with friends, we can easily be tempted to stay out later and keep the night going, and endure the next day sleep-deprived or reliant on a few cups of coffee to make sense of the day. By choosing to stay up late, we are creating a knock-on effect that will have a negative impact on our ability to be present and attentive throughout the next day, and so we must learn to be vigilant about our rest and ensure that we prioritize our self-sustainability and wellbeing over a single night's temptations, no matter how fun it may seem at the time.

For us to live well, we must learn how to rest well. Rest is the act of restoration and reprieve, and when we prioritize our rest, we are refilling our capacity, allowing us to move through each day with clarity and agency. When we are well rested, we have the ability to do anything; every moment is ours to own.

Now, you may say, 'It is not possible for me to be home and in bed by midnight, my life does not suit this same rhythm.' You may have a night job or a newborn baby, or you may have a small puppy, like I do, named Gus, that keeps you up at night. And this is OK. Do not feel that you are inadequate if your situation is different, perhaps see the lesson in the story and apply it to your life as you can. If you go to bed later, then sleep in longer; if you are unable to be home before midnight, then simply be purposeful in how you end the day. Do not be afraid to ask the people in your life to support your time to rest. My only hope is that you make rest a priority and ensure that it is non-negotiable and is not sacrificed to the other activities in your life.

These days, I find that there is nothing more exciting than a good night's rest, and the older I get, the truer this becomes. Perhaps this, too, can be a great joy in your life, and a reminder that there is nothing in life more important than a well-rested soul.

Quiet is the choice
to remove distractions

WHAT COMES
FROM WEAKNESS

How often do you spend time on the things you're not so good at? How often do you put your attention to the aspects of your life that need work and the dedication of your time? This is the practice of cultivating the opposite, a perspective that is counter-intuitive to the progress of life. Growing up, we are taught to lean into what we excel at; we nurture our skills and celebrate our offering to the world. If you are good at writing, you should write books; if you are great at sports, you should be an athlete; if you can cook and prepare a delicious meal, you should become a chef. Life has become about being good at what we are good at.

And so, throughout our lives, we cultivate our skills and strong capabilities because they give us a strong sense of identity and purpose that in turn give us a certain place within society. This is also so we can be seen as valuable to the people around us and a contributor to our communities. Our lives and abilities are specialized, rather than generalized; we are praised for our productivity. But how often do we lean the other way? Away from what we excel at towards that which challenges us?

There is so much growth when we cultivate the opposite in our actions for it gifts us real and honest perspective. When we lean away from our familiarities and dedicate our attention and consideration towards that which is new or different, we cultivate a true evolution in balance, and self-awareness of our perceived weaknesses. If, at a younger age, you realized you were great at maths, your life may have been guided along a logical and analytical path; if you excelled at art and creative endeavours, then perhaps you were guided along this colourful path. Inevitably, your skills become your identity, so if you are analytical, you may not think of yourself as creative; if you are artistic, you may not consider yourself logical. But what if we are, and just simply haven't nurtured these qualities within us? When we choose to cultivate the opposite and move away from familiarity, we are choosing a path to regain the balance of a well-rounded and fully experienced life.

For us to grow, we must lean towards our discomforts. The more we do this, even in smaller moments, the more we find that challenges in our lives become less challenging. In time, our capabilities and capacity increase. We must always make way for our weaknesses, for they teach us how to find our way back to a balanced way of being.

Growth only
happens when
permission is
granted

NOURISH WHAT REMAINS

I am lucky to have a garden at the back of my home. It is not large, but it is lush and, throughout the year, the garden springs into new life, especially when there is a lot of rain, which helps to sprout many plants, flowers, weeds and more.

Looking out the window each morning, I can see a jungle of life in bloom, and it is a beautiful sight to gaze upon. But if it is left unattended, it will quickly become overgrown and untidy, and nearly impossible to walk around in and enjoy the space. And so, as in most domestic green spaces, the trees need to be trimmed and the overgrowth and the weeds pulled out.

Now, on one such occasion, our garden was so overgrown we could not even distinguish the bushes from the trees. It looked like one gigantic green abyss. The gardener who would typically visit weekly hadn't come in a few months for various reasons, and so when he finally came to clear the garden, we had unknowingly grown quite attached to the way it had become.

It was obvious that the garden needed to be trimmed back; it was unmanaged and, in fact, it was so overgrown that two local foxes had started using it as a nesting ground because of the cover from the sun and the privacy the tall grass and weeds offered. Our backyard had transformed from a useable garden space into a forested habitat. However, surprisingly, the idea of change was unsettling; we had grown so familiar with how it was now that for a moment we were unsure if we really wanted the work to be done. Eventually, the gardener explained that it was necessary to trim the overgrowth back; it wasn't beneficial for the trees and garden space to let it grow untended, and over time, if we left it, it would cause damage to the surrounding space.

And so, reluctantly, we agreed, and over the course of the after-noon our garden was transformed back into a useable space that we could again enjoy. We had forgotten how wonderful some of the smaller tress were; they had been overshadowed by some of the larger ones. We hadn't seen the cherry blossom or plum trees for many months now and, to our luck, they were in bloom. When it was all done, we were so grateful; we had our garden back and enjoyed looking forward to sitting on the grass again and reading in the sunshine. The foxes even returned from time to time to lie in the freshly cut grass. I suppose they, too, appreciated the trimming.

The following month, when the gardener returned to tend the garden again, he asked, 'Do you miss the jungle?', and for a moment I paused with a puzzled look before answering; for a split second, I had completely forgotten about the garden over-growth. 'Not for one minute,' I replied, smiling. 'I have enjoyed many naps in the garden since the last time you were here.' He smiled back and chuckled.

I suppose the lesson in all this is that, often, as humans, we can easily forget the past if the present is more enriching. Things that happened last week or maybe last month can quickly lose their appeal as they become mundane memories, easily replaced by what is now and what is new.

But there are also times in our lives when the opposite can happen, perhaps a break-up or an injury or illness that significantly changes your lifestyle. We cannot let go of our misery and are unable to find any positivity in our new situation or circumstances. Now, in some cases, these changes are not choices that we make voluntarily, but the lesson is still the same. In times of significant shift or, in my case, a clearing of the weeds, there is no value in dwelling on what we have lost, for it does not benefit how we live presently. We must instead allow ourselves the time to nourish only what remains, and go, and grow, from there.

We do not clear the weeds only
to miss them when they are gone

STEP TEN
THE CROWN FOLD

We are near the end now, and all that remains are small folds. This is the step where great truth is transformed and our crane begins to take shape. This is the crown fold. To begin, start by holding one side of your crane with your thumb and index finger; with your other thumb and first finger, unfold the chopstick leg back to a straight position and begin to gently spread the top and bottom layers of the flaps. Do this delicately, making it wide enough to reveal the space between the layers to invite in a new fold to be created within it. Here will be the nook for the crane's neck and crowned head.

Next, run your right thumb down the crevice of this space and, at the same time, delicately slide your first finger behind the top part of the leg until the fingers meet on opposite sides of the same paper leg. Use your thumb as the anchor and fold the leg outwards, revealing the crease that was folded in step 9. This is often called an inverted or 'inside-out' fold. As the neck starts to take shape, seal the fold by closing the outer flaps back into their original position, running your fingers along both sides of the crane's neck, from base to crown. Things are starting to take shape. When you are ready, begin the second leg. This is the fold that will become the crane's tail feather. When you have completed this second side, you will arrive at the folded crown, in honour of the Tancho, the Japanese red-crowned crane, which is said to be the inspiration behind all folded paper cranes.

SIMPLICITY
REMOVING DISTRACTIONS

Humans have a way of gravitating towards complexity, always striving for more, never fulfilled, always needing. We have become masterful at coping with the quantity of life, and feel that if we are not doing more, we are living less. But this is not the way; a fulfilled life is defined by quality, not quantity. We must reduce the temptations of a busy world and move away from the expectations of the ego. Simplicity is an evolution we find in time, it is the practice of removing unneeded distractions and recognizing the gift of less.

IN TIME,
EVERYTHING QUIETENS

I have never been fond of speaking too many words. I try, where possible, to only speak when spoken to, and always try to keep my talks to a minimum when teaching a gathering of students. I am also not one for big groups or small talk, perhaps this is why meditation is so appealing to me – not because I am averse to meaningful conversation, but because I believe that there are many moments when words are simply not needed, even if they are always expected. Some people cannot bear the sound of silence; for them, it can be a deafening experience, so they will always choose to fill empty space with empty words.

And so, I have spent time observing others in these situations so that I may understand why, and I have come to realize that there are a few reasons why people do not cope well with the sound of silence.

The first is that people want to be liked and appreciated by others, and in moments of silence we can easily be misunderstood or misrepresented and a disconnect can develop. So, we use our words to elevate how we see the world and how others should understand who we are. By nature, humans are very boastful. We share our accomplishments, talk about our successes and aim to prove our worthiness to the people around us, and the more we speak, the more we are able to shape our identities to suit our prescribed realities.

The second reason is that we are afraid of being alone. Many people cannot bear the idea of being by themselves, without the company of others, and silence can prompt a feeling of loneliness, whereas words and spirited exchanges allow us to feel a meaningful connection. I find that some people will prolong their conversations far longer than needed so that they can keep a connection going and abate any feelings of loneliness or aloneness.

And finally, the third reason is that we are uncomfortable simply being in a state of non-doing. We have become victims of distraction, unable to appreciate moments when we need not be stimulated by our words or interactions. When we are speaking or in conversation with someone else, we are in a constant exchange of stimulation, but when we are quiet, and no words are shared, we are left in what remains: bliss.

TAKE WHAT YOU NEED,
LEAVE WHAT YOU DO NOT

Growing up in Los Angeles, my family spent summer vacations and other holidays visiting grandparents and other relatives back home in New Zealand, where our family is from. Living so far away, our family would take every possible opportunity to visit, and during school holidays we would also make the trip abroad. With such a long way to go, and luggage at a premium on flights, we were only ever allowed one bag each to travel with. Everything we wanted to pack had to fit in a single case.

One year when I was around nine or ten, I had received a new skateboard for my birthday, so I decided that I would bring it with me and show off my new skills to my cousins, as I was very proud of it and I enjoyed riding around the streets and footpaths, weaving in and out of rubbish bins and parked cars. Now, in my family, there was only one rule when packing: do not pack a bag you cannot carry. You could bring with you whatever you wanted, literally anything, but whatever you chose to bring was your responsibility alone to carry for the entire trip. My father made it a point that no one else could help. There was no sympathy for overambitious decisions.

Before the trip, my mother tried on multiple occasions to convince me that it was not a good idea to bring the skateboard with me, saying I would tire of it and that it would end up being more trouble than it was worth. I, of course, disagreed and packed it in my bag anyway. As we loaded up the car and headed to the airport, my fate was sealed, and for the next two weeks it was mine alone to manage.

Inevitably, in the excitement of the trip, seeing all our relatives, playing with cousins and spending time on the road between cities, my skateboard was used maybe once, or twice, perhaps. There were many occasions throughout the trip where I attempted to play the victim, asking my parents to carry it for me, but they lovingly declined and reminded me of the decision I had made at the start of the trip. This was a life lesson that played out in real time. I would complain every time we had to pack up and move on to the next place and, each and every time, I would be reminded by my brother, 'Don't pack a bag you can't carry,' as he laughed and poked fun at me, like a big brother would. There was one occasion where my father asked if I wanted to get rid of the skateboard and leave it behind with one of my cousins. He said that if I chose to leave it behind, it would surely lighten my load. I declined and persisted, in misery. Needless to say, when we eventually made it back to Los Angeles, I was happy to be done with the trip.

I hope this story gave you a little chuckle, as it does me every time I look back on it. If only I knew then what I know now, but I suppose that is easy to say all these years later. And while this trip will never be the highlight of my childhood travels, the lesson and learning that I gained from it have stayed with me a lifetime.

On most occasions in life, we are in control of the choices we make and the things we choose to carry with us on our way, and I am speaking both of literal things but also of emotional ones. If we crowd our lives with too many personal items and material things, we will slowly weigh ourselves down and become unable to travel freely or unencumbered. Likewise, we must try not to carry unneeded emotional baggage or the weight of others' expectations, as these, too, can be heavy and paralysing if not intentionally eased.

For me, my mistake was a two-week misfortune, one that I have still not forgotten, but in life and emotions, if we are not careful or intentional, our misery could last much longer, and so we must always remember to lighten our load and pack wisely for the journey that we are on. Take only what you need and leave what you do not.

I suppose this is also a good reminder that mothers always know best.

Do not pack a bag
you cannot carry

The secret to stillness
is realizing that it is a
pleasure, not a punishment

LEARN TO SPEND
TIME ALONE

Why are we afraid of being alone? Often, when we hear the word 'alone', it can have a negative connotation, with a sense of unwantedness or disconnection. At the same time, when we are alone, we can fear that we are missing out on the excitement of life, on special moments and meaningful connections.

So, what is the point of being alone? What is the value of finding separation? These days, life is dictated so heavily by social situations and interactions, constant stimulus and endless engagement. We are always online, in communication, around people; our proximity is quite immediate to so many things and so many voices. And this can be suffocating, so when we choose to step away, to find moments to be alone – five minutes, ten minutes, an hour – it gives us the chance to breathe again, literally and figuratively. We de-stimulate, we can digest the interactions of living. We can reflect, we can recognize how the world around us has an impact on us, and the best remedy for this is quiet moments away from the noise of life and the company of other people.

Being alone is not missing out, it is in fact about tuning in, it is about discovering the enjoyment of our own company and realizing that we are not without.

These days, the more I travel, the more I yearn for time alone, not to remove myself from the joys of life, but to feel that I can engage more meaningfully. At times, the further we step away from the world, the closer we step towards ourselves, the more we can be comfortable being in solitude, the more it becomes familiar and fulfilling. Quietude can gift us a feeling of safety, a feeling that is necessary, essential and empowering in a busy and noisy world. Learning to be alone is a feeling of coming home.

One of my favourite things to do is to take myself to lunch and enjoy a meal in my own company. I remember, when I was younger, this would be the most frightening and scary thing that I could think to do, to be seen out in the world by myself, thinking I was being judged by others, no one whose time I was worth. But since then I have found this to be untrue. There is so much joy in keeping our own company; it is a gift of absolute freedom.

In time, simplicity is
an inevitable result

Mastery is the result of
repetition, simplicity is
the result of recognition

STEP ELEVEN
THE WISDOM FOLD

We are almost there, but do not rush. There are still a few steps left to fold, and they should be enjoyed completely. The next step is the wisdom fold. Let us use this fold to breathe life into the creases. This penultimate fold can be a meticulous one, as the fold is small and delicate, but that is fitting, as it is the fold that sparks the gift of life to our majestic creature.

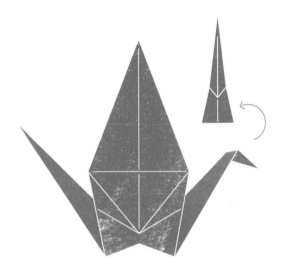

To create this fold, start by running your thumb up the crease of the neck to create some space between the fold. Measure with your thumb one centimetre from the top of the neck and place your first finger on the back of the inverted fold. Pinch gently and fold downwards; this should create the shape of the crane's head and crown. You must be gentle here, because it can be easy to crumple the end. As you create this crowned fold, you will need to invert the crease to create a pronounced shape for the head. It can be unforgiving at first, so do not fret if it does not go exactly to plan.

JOY

GRACIOUS REFINEMENT

As we arrive here at the final step, I hope that this book has served you well. In my life, I have learned that joy is a practice of continuous discovery and gracious refinement, and that our lives are simply a gift of self-awareness, each moment unfolding with new inspirations and inward connection.

Happiness just is; a warmth that radiates within but illuminates outwards, and one that we can only truly find when we walk our own path with small and many steps.

WHEN GROWING OLD,
HOW EASILY WE FORGET

Throughout my life, I have been lucky to sit with many scholars and spiritual teachers, however, I find that my greatest insights come from interactions with children, as they see the world with such curious eyes and inquisitive minds. Children have a way of seeing unconditional beauty and speaking with honest brutality, they are untarnished by the temptations of growing up and remain pure in their youthfulness. When speaking to children, I have found that they never sugar-coat their observations to better suit a prescribed identity or predis-position, and their honesty is refreshing in a world that has become far too familiar with manipulated truths that serve our constructed realities and curative fantasies.

Now, I do not have any children of my own, and so when I am around friends and family with small children or find myself at an event or gathering where children are present, I will always make time to speak to them and ask genuine questions. Sometimes, the answers are jumbled and meaningless, and if this is the case, it is a delight just to see their exuberant spirit, but on other occasions, and more often than you may think, their responses are deeply insightful and profound, simply because they do not waste their words or soften their subtitles.

In all my exchanges with children, I have come to recognize these four qualities which, to me, are why their words carry so much wisdom.

First, children, up until a certain age, are not conflicted by the expectations of others. They simply do not care what they say, or who it may offend; they do not soften their thoughts in order to respect or protect others' feelings. This is why insights from children can be both beautiful and brutal. It is likely that we have all been on the receiving end of the critical eye of a child, and there is nothing more humbling than a child who tells you that they do not like your shoes, or that you are being bossy, or that you smell funny when you have simply tried on a new fragrance. But children do not say these things to be hurtful, their words are not spiteful, they are simply sharing with honesty how they see the world unfolding. When this happens, smile and laugh; do not be upset. It is our responsibility to encourage the spirit of children, for it is a quality, sadly, that life will in time dampen, and we do not need to help quicken the pace.

Secondly, children are simple creatures, not by choice, but simply by the way they are. They know very little about life, and their understanding of the world is still minimal, much of it yet to be understood. Their lives consist mainly of sleeping, eating, learning and playing; this is itself a joyful life that we may all agree upon. Thankfully, they are not burdened with the complexity of adolescence or adult life. What we learn from this is that when we act from a place of simplicity, then the only things that matter are the things that are essential to living well and enjoying life; ego, attachment and intricacy have no place in these moments.

Thirdly, children are incapable of living outside the present. They do not burden themselves with the misery of yesterday or what will happen tomorrow; they are incapable of that kind of torment and self-conscious projection. If it is not happening now, it is not happening at all. Children simply ebb and flow with each moment, always attentive to the right here, right now.

And, finally, children will choose happiness above all else. They do not care for the status of life, they simply want to enjoy every moment completely. Whereas, as adults, we can easily manipulate our happiness with obligation, expectation or moderation; we let our joy be subjective or pre-prescribed. For children, if there is ice cream to eat, they will not think twice, or if there is a puddle to splash in, they will jump right in. They do not think of the mess it makes or the cold they might catch, they do not weigh the risk or return; these are only the misfortunes of growing up. How easily we replace our joy with complexity. And so we must always remember the wisdom of children and remind ourselves that life is best lived without expectation. Live simply, stay present and choose only the things that make you truly happy, right now, in this moment.

Life is not the act of discovery,
but the act of remembering

A TRAVELLING PRAYER

Each day I remember that I have come this far,
Not to arrive, but to discover what unfolds along the way.
But I am in no rush, for I have nowhere I need to be.

Do not be tempted by the rising tide,
Go forth with gentleness, unconditionally, completely,
Be patient and slow your wandering step.

This life is a gift we must walk graciously,
Give yourself permission to feel the breeze,
Freedom is on the horizon.

Walk the mountains, and take the path out to the sea,
Be curious about what lies beyond the sunset,
The quiet waves are not our only serenity.

Rise each day so we may remember,
Love relentlessly, offer forgiveness,
This path must be walked tenderly.

Time is a gift,
Let it wash away the past,
Let all that remains, be our joy.

But still I am in no rush.

A bird cannot
fly without an
open heart

IN THE END, WE FIND
NEW BEGINNING

In life, all good things will come to an end, but in every ending we must not see these moments as absolute but instead as joy fulfilled so that new moments may unfold.

At the back of this book, you will find some blank pages. I have left them in so you have further space to wander and discover. Let this be a gift of new beginnings. If you are inspired to use them to fold, be gentle as you remove them, so that it does not tear the binding of the book or cause the spine to unravel. Or perhaps you could use them to share your own stories and gentle wisdoms. If you are feeling creative, let your imagination and pen run free.

Whatever you choose to do with these pages, gift yourself this space to slow down and just see what takes shape.

Even the most beautiful
sunset will always make
way for the rising sun

Joy is the result of needing
nothing, yet having everything

STEP TWELVE
THE FINAL FOLD

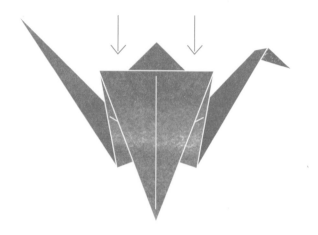

You have arrived at the final step, and while it may be the last step for this crane, it is only just the beginning. As you finish your folds, appreciate the journey that has brought you here. Now is the time to spread your wings and fly. To fold down the wings, simply hold the base of the crane in one hand while the thumb and first finger of your other hand trace down the front and back of the top wing. As your index finger finds the base of the inside wing, let this be the point where you create the fold. Gently turn the fold down and use your thumbs to crease it firmly. If it is helpful, place your crane down on the table to use the hard surface behind to ensure the fold is deep and meaningful. And, when you are ready, simply flip the crane over and fold the remaining wing down to match the wing from the first side. This is the first flap of the wings as the crane prepares to fly. This is the crane's new beginning. I always find both excitement and inspiration in this moment.

The final stage of folding your paper crane is, surprisingly, not a fold at all, it is instead an act of unfolding. Turn the crane to face forward so it can look to the future, hold the tip of each wing and very gently spread the wings apart. This final step will breathe life into the body of the bird and gift your crane the spark of life. You have arrived, and your paper crane is finished. If you are still holding it, perhaps place it down on the table and sit back. Take a moment to really see and appreciate the efforts of your practice. I hope that there is joy within you, and I hope that this journey was time well spent.

This is the gift of Senbazuru: a mindful practice that allows us to slow down and turn inwards to discover our way along the path to hope, healing and happiness.

Now is the time to start your journey of folding one thousand paper cranes. It may seem like a daunting task when you begin, but remember, you do not need to go at it alone. Folding your Senbazuru is a journey of self discovery; each fold should be deliberate and purposeful. And though misguided folds will occur along the way, this should not be unexpected, but do not see them as mistakes, for they are simply moments to learn from and to let go. The beauty of this journey is that each crane is a new beginning, each new fold inspired by the ones that have come before. Do not rush this process, you have plenty of time for this wishful intention to unfold.

ONWARD

CREATE YOUR OWN SENBAZURU

I will write peace on your
wings and you will fly all
over the world

Sadako Sasaki

THE FEATHER OF HOPE

As legend says, if one thousand cranes are folded within a single year, a single wish is granted. Often this wish is made at the start of the journey as a guiding inspiration for the many folds that follow. Some traditions say that your wish should not be said out loud; instead, it should be kept in the heart, not on the tongue. As for me, before I begin to fold one thousand cranes, I start first by folding a paper feather that holds my wishful intention. I call it, *the Feather of Hope.*

Using a single sheet of paper, I will write down my wish, taking a moment to honour the practice, and then I will fold it into a *Feather of Hope*, which I keep nearby as I fold. If you would like, you can do this now, too. This has become one of my most favourite personal traditions when folding one thousand paper cranes. Creating a Senbazuru is no small task, but do not fear the journey ahead, simply enjoy this new beginning. In many cultures around the world, a single feather represents strength, wisdom, freedom and hope, and so I hold these beliefs within your folded feather as you begin to fold. At times, in between folds, I hold it in my hand so that I can feel its meaning in my heart.

When you come to complete your Senbazuru, you may choose, like I do, to hang this feather from the central hook where all the threads meet, as a symbol of the journey from the beginning to the end. *The Feather of Hope* will always hang above the cranes as guidance for the flock so that they always remember their purpose as they take flight with wishful intentions.

When sitting down to fold your feather, choose your colour with care. Let it resonate with the qualities of the wish without giving away what it is. For example, if your wish is for a deep and loving relationship, then the paper will be red, or if your wish is for long life and good fortune, the feather will be yellow.

To create your own feather, you do not need to learn any new folds, simply complete steps 1–8 in folding a paper crane. Once these eight folds are completed, the shape will resemble a single feather, so there is nothing more you need to learn. Once you have folded your feather, hang it upside down so that its tip is pointing upwards and its tail can fly in the wind.

CONSTRUCTING
YOUR SENBAZURU

After you have folded one thousand paper cranes, you will need to construct them into a flock. There are two different paths to completing the journey; you may find one more favourable than the other.

Fold, then fly (fold first, then thread) – Many people will prefer this method for folding a Senbazuru: first fold all one thousand cranes, then string them together so they can fly as one hanging ornament. On some days throughout the year, you may prefer to fold many, and on others you may fold only a few or even none. Know it is not necessary to fold every single day; instead, find your own rhythm along the way. Now, there will be some of you who prefer a steadier cadence. If this is you, then fold two or three cranes every day and you will reach a thousand within the year.

Folding in flocks (forty folds at a time) – Fold your cranes in a batch of forty; perhaps you may prefer to fold all the cranes of one colour at a time before moving on. Once you have finished your forty folded cranes, string them together and tie the thread from your centre point. Repeat this process a total of twenty-five times until you have reached one thousand. If you want to create a thread that hangs more neatly, do not fold the wings down; let them stay unfolded so they can nestle more comfortably with the others. Once you have folded and threaded all the strings of cranes, attach them to a single hook so that you may hang them as one.

The red thread

A red thread is a symbolic idea in many cultures and ideologies, and it often symbolizes the connection between concepts, people or traditions. Red, as we know, is an empowering colour, vibrant and passionate like the sun. When stringing together a Senbazuru, a red thread connects all the many cranes together in unity and community. It is literally and figuratively the red thread that unites the flock during such a heartfelt journey.

The golden bead

When it is time to thread your paper cranes together, use a single bead tied to the end of a strong thread to begin. This is, of course, so your birds do not fly away. You may use any bead, but I like to use a single golden bead at the base of each thread. Traditionally, gold is the colour of good fortune, and so starting each thread with this quality is a meaningful beginning.

A PLACE TO CALL HOME

Once completed, a Senbazuru needs a meaningful home or place to adorn. Some people will hang them in a window or a room of their home that feels like it honours the intention. Others will often take them to a place of worship or personal significance, such as a temple, community centre or the home of an elderly relative, and hang them there to share a respectful offering to someone or something. In times of tragedy or hardship, Senbazurus are offered as a sign of hopefulness and peace at memorials, museums or places of special significance. At times of celebration, like weddings or to mark a significant accomplishment, Senbazurus are gifted as joyful offerings. Often, cranes are shared in the same manner as one would bring a bouquet of flowers for occasions of both happiness and sadness.

Inevitably, the journey to one thousand cranes is a process that unfolds one step at a time, and for anyone choosing to walk this path, know that it is always a sincere endeavour. I myself enjoy the practice of dedicating myself to something mindful for a prolonged period. For people who live busy and stressful lives, this journey will be a revelation.

So now is the time for you to begin. Take what you have learned and let it inspire your journey onwards. I wish you well. As you begin, go forth gently. Behind you now are many gentle wisdoms to guide you on your way. Hold them close and revisit them often, but they can only take you so far. Ahead of you is a path that only you can wander. Let this excite you, but not rush you.

Remember always that the path to happiness is found with small steps and many steps along the way, and the most beautiful journey is one taken at a gentle pace.

Take with you this last remembrance, that in the end, we always find a new beginning.

Let this be yours

HOW TO FOLD
A PAPER CRANE

STEP 1
THE DIAGONAL FOLD

STEP 2
THE BOOK FOLD

STEP 3
THE SANDWICH FOLD

STEP 4
THE KITE FOLD

STEP 5
THE TRIANGLE FOLD

STEP 6
THE SEASHELL FOLD

STEP 7
THE DIAMOND FOLD

STEP 8
THE FOLDED FEATHER

STEP 9
THE CHOPSTICK FOLD

STEP 10
THE CROWN FOLD

STEP 11
THE WISDOM FOLD

STEP 12
THE FINAL FOLD

When we remove the
distractions of life all
that remains is joy

MICHAEL JOSEPH

UK | USA | Canada | Ireland | Australia
India | New Zealand | South Africa

Michael Joseph is part of the Penguin Random House
group of companies whose addresses can be found at
global.penguinrandomhouse.com

First published 2021
001

Set in SangBleu and Bluu Next
Reproduction by Altaimage, London
Printed by Livonia Print, Latvia

The authorized representative in the EEA is
Penguin Random House Ireland, Morrison Chambers,
32 Nassau Street, Dublin D02 YH68

A CIP catalogue record for this book
is available from the British Library

ISBN: 978-0-241-51139-8

www.greenpenguin.co.uk